P9-BJB-181

At Issue

| Military Recruiters

Other Books in the At Issue Series:

At Issue

Military Recruiters

Lauri Harding, Book Editor

GREENHAVEN PRESS

An imprint of Thomson Gale, a part of The Thomson Corporation

THOMSON

GALE

Detroit • New York • San Francisco • New Haven, Conn. • Waterville, Maine • London

Christine Nasso, *Publisher*
Elizabeth Des Chenes, *Managing Editor*

© 2008 The Gale Group.

Star logo is a trademark and Gale and Greenhaven Press are registered trademarks used herein under license.

For more information, contact:
Greenhaven Press
27500 Drake Rd.
Farmington Hills, MI 48331-3535
Or you can visit our Internet site at http://www.gale.com

ALL RIGHTS RESERVED
No part of this work covered by the copyright hereon may be reproduced or used in any form or by any means—graphic, electronic, or mechanical, including photocopying, record-ing, taping, Web distribution, or information storage retrieval systems—without the written permission of the publisher.

Articles in Greenhaven Press anthologies are often edited for length to meet page require-ments. In addition, original titles of these works are changed to clearly present the main thesis and to explicitly indicate the author's opinion. Every effort is made to ensure that Greenhaven Press accurately reflects the original intent of the authors. Every effort has been made to trace the owners of copyrighted material.

LIBRARY OF CONGRESS CATALOGING-IN-PUBLICATION DATA

Military recruiters / Lauri Harding, book editor.
    p. cm. -- (At issue)
    Includes bibliographical references and index.
    ISBN-13: 978-0-7377-3787-5 (hardcover)
    ISBN-13: 978-0-7377-3788-2 (pbk.)
    1. United States--Armed Forces--Recruiting, enlistment, etc. 2. United States--ArmedForces--Recruiting, enlistment, etc.--Iraq War, 2003- 3. Military service, Voluntary-- United States. 4. Draft--United States. I. Harding, Lauri.
    UB323.M55 2007
    355.2'23620973--dc22

                                     2007037478

ISBN-10: 0-7377-3787-5 (hardcover)
ISBN-10: 0-7377-3788-3 (pbk.)

Printed in the United States of America
10 9 8 7 6 5 4 3 2 1

Contents

Introduction

Jessica Faustner was only seventeen years old and a few months short of graduating from Northampton Area High School near Allentown, Pennsylvania when she enlisted in the Pennsylvania Army National Guard in 2005. Described by reporter Lawrence Hardy as a bright but mediocre student who was "more infatuated with boys than schoolwork," Faustner began attending the Guard's monthly drill weekends at Allentown's National Guard Armory, but suddenly stopped before her final required session and went into hiding.

Faustner would later go public with accusations that a Guard recruiter had enticed her into enlisting with an offer of sending her through nursing school before she would be deployed overseas. Through her attorney, she further alleged that the recruiter used other deceptive practices to get her and her parents to sign her enlistment papers. According to Faustner, after enlisting she learned at a meeting of new recruits that she had a 90 percent chance of being deployed to Iraq after basic training. So she went AWOL (absent without leave) instead. "You know, a 17-year-old girl should be thinking about her prom and her graduation, not about going to Iraq. She was just misled all the way around," her attorney, John Roberts, told reporters.

Back in Allentown, a big showdown between Faustner (in hiding and speaking through her attorney) and the National Guard (threatening to prosecute her and compel her to report for duty) dominated the local media for weeks. Captain Cory Angell, a spokesperson for the National Guard, contended that Faustner's assumption of immediate deployment to Iraq was wrong. "She, at minimum, would be non-deployable until her second year of college," Angell commented.

Faustner's allegations of wrongdoing by her recruiter are not uncommon. The war in Iraq created heightened demand for military manpower by 2005. Men and women serving in the active-duty military, the Reserves, and the National Guard could all expect to be sent overseas to fight. With casualties mounting and popular support for the war in decline, military recruiters were under pressure.

In fact, Faustner's complaint coincided with a massive U.S. Army "stand down" (a one-day halt in all recruiting activities) to review recruiting practices used by the military across the nation. This was mostly in response to recurring media reports of fraud and deception, and a measurable rise in claims alleging recruiter misconduct. Between fiscal years 2004 and 2005, the military reviewed more than 11,000 cases of alleged deception, coercion, or other abuse by military recruiters.

In Faustner's case, a full investigation was conducted and a staff judge advocate concluded that her accusations were not substantiated. "Our recruiting command says he [the recruiter] did everything to the letter, to the 'T' perfect," said Angell. But in other cases misunderstandings between military recruiters and their prospective enlistees have been substantiated, and are increasingly common as America's citizens grapple with conflicting notions of honor, duty, patriotism, and their fears of being sent into battle.

There are recruiters deserving of criticism for their role in painting an unrealistic picture of military service, or stoking the fire of patriotism that feeds unrealistic expectations of military conflict and its dangers. Some have gone as far as to intentionally deceive. They have taken the innocent enthusiasm of many and turned it into sour resentment.

On the other hand, honorable and undeserving recruiters have themselves been victims of counter-recruitment extremism (particularly on college campuses) involving ransacked offices, blood thrown through smashed windows, recruiting vehicles set on fire, and office door locks jammed with powerful glue. Other recruiters, lawfully dispatched to set up recruiting booths at local high schools or college campuses, have been met with massive anti-war demonstrations and protests. Students have blocked access to recruiting booths for interested students wanting information, and many recruiters have been falsely charged of wrongful conduct or statement.

Recruiters often serve as "fall guys," taking criticism as the result of unpopular wars, unpopular recruiting policies and practices, and unpopular political administrations or agendas. Many in the general public who oppose recruiters would do so for these reasons even if there were no cases of recruiters behaving improperly.

In the end, most Americans believe that the United States needs a competent and committed military. The all-volunteer force relies on recruiters to make this a reality, therefore protesting them for doing their jobs can be counterproductive. As Ken Harbaugh, a former Navy Pilot and student at Yale Law School, put it in a commentary on *National Public Radio:*

> Every year the law school sends some of its brightest graduates to work in the Justice Department and the State Department. Yale certainly doesn't endorse every practice of those organizations, but it understands that by working with them it is much more likely to influence their policies for the better. . . .
>
> Imagine if America's elite universities had obstructed recruiting efforts during World War II. God knows there were decent reasons then. Just consider the appalling treatment of blacks in uniform. But Yale and others sent their best to fight and, in doing so, helped improve the character of our armed forces.

It is this conflict that makes military recruiters and recruitment such a controversial issue. Justified or not, military recruiters will continue to face charges of deception and abusive practices so long as they remain the primary means of convincing young Americans to join the armed forces.

1

Military Recruiters Charm Impressionable Youth Into Risky Business

William Ayers

William Ayers is a professor of education and senior university scholar at the University of Illinois at Chicago. He is a published author in the field of education.

Military recruiters influence vulnerable teenagers by taking advantage of their desire to fit in, aggression, and sense of invincibility. The prospect of becoming a member of an identifiable group with a distinctive uniform, combined with a shared mission and grand purpose, is highly attractive to teens. Moreover, the military culture especially appeals to lower-income youths with less opportunity for varied futures. This makes the Junior Reserve Officers' Training Corps (JROTC, the high school version of ROTC) a popular choice in many schools. As a result, high schools have become battlefields for the hearts and minds of our youth.

In her book, *Purple Hearts*, documentary photographer Nina Berman presents 40 photographs—two each of 20 U.S. veterans of the American war in Iraq—plus a couple accompanying paragraphs of commentary from each vet in his or her own words.

Their comments cohere around their service, their sacrifice, their suffering. The Purple Heart binds them together—

William Ayers, "Hearts and Minds: Military Recruitment and the High School Battlefield," *Education Digest*, vol. 71, May 2006, pp. 594–599. Reproduced by permission.

this award is their common experience, this distinction is what they embrace and what embraces them. This is what they live with.

Youthful Stories

Their views on war, on their time in arms, on where they hope they are headed with their lives, are various; their ways of making sense about the U.S. military mission, wildly divergent.

Josh Olson, 24 years old, begins: "We bent over backwards for these people, but they ended up screwing us over, stabbing us in the back. A lot of them, I mean, they're going to have to be killed. . . . As Americans we've taken it upon ourselves to almost cure the world's problems I guess, give everybody else a chance. I guess that's how we're good-hearted." He's missing his right leg now and was presented with his Purple Heart at Walter Reed Military Hospital by President Bush himself. He feels it all—pride, anger, loss.

Jermaine Lewis, 23, grew up in a Chicago neighborhood where "death has always been around." At basic training, "they break you down and then they try to build you up." To him, the "reasons for going to war were bogus, but we were right to go in there."

The vets are all young. Several recall deciding to enlist when much younger still, more innocent, more vulnerable, but feeling somehow invincible. Says Lewis: "I've been dealing with the military since I was a sophomore in high school. They came to the school like six times a year, all military branches. They had a recruiting station like a block from our high school. It was just right there."

Tyson Johnson III, 22, wanted out of the poverty and death he saw all around him. His life was going nowhere, he thought, so he signed on: "And here I am, back here . . . I don't know where it's going to end up." Joseph Mosner enrolled at 19: "There was nothing out there. There was no good jobs so I figured this would have been a good thing." Frederick Allen thought war would be "jumping out of planes." He joined when recruiters came to his high school. "I thought it would be fun."

Add the need to prove oneself to be a macho, strong, tough, capable person, combined with an unrealistic calculus of vulnerability and a constricted sense of options specifically in poor and working-class communities—all of this creates the toxic mix in a young person's head that can be a military recruiter's dream.

Adam Zaremba, 20, also enlisted while still in high school: "The recruiter called the house, he was actually looking for my brother and he happened to get me. I think it was because I didn't want to do homework for a while, and then I don't know, you get to wear a cool uniform. It just went on from there. I still don't even understand a lot about the Army."

His Purple Heart seemed like a good thing from a distance, "but then when it happens you realize that you have to do something, or something has to happen to you in order to get it."

Creating an Appealing Image

Military recruiting in high schools has been a mainstay of the so-called all-volunteer armed forces from the start. High school kids are at an age when being a member of an identifiable group with a grand mission and a shared spirit—and never underestimate a distinctive uniform—is of exaggerated importance, which gang recruiters in big cities note with interest and exploit with skill.

Kathy Dobie (in "AWOL in America," in Harper's, March 2005), quoting a military historian, notes that "basic training has been essentially the same in every army in every age, because it works with the same raw material that's always been there in teenage boys: a fair amount of aggression, a strong tendency to hang around in groups, and an absolute desperate desire to fit in."

Being cool and going along with the crowd are big things. Add the need to prove oneself to be a macho, strong, tough, capable person, combined with an unrealistic calculus of vulnerability and a constricted sense of options specifically in poor and working-class communities—all of this creates the toxic mix in a young person's head that can be a military recruiter's dream.

One of the most effective recruitment tools is Junior Reserve Officers' Training Corps (JROTC), the high school version of ROTC established by an act of Congress in 1916 "to develop citizenship and responsibility in young people." JROTC is now experiencing the most rapid expansion in its history. . . .

There is no doubt that JROTC programs target poor, black, and Latino kids without the widest range of options to begin with.

JROTC and MSCC [Middle School Cadet Corps] defenders claim the goal is leadership and citizen development, dropout prevention or simply the fun of dressing up and parading around. Skeptics note that Pentagon money for these programs provides needed resources for starving public schools and ask why the military has become such an important route to adequate school funding. . . .

Selective Recruiting

There is no doubt that JROTC programs target poor, black, and Latino kids without the widest range of options to begin with. Recruiters know where to go: Whitney Young High School, a large, selective magnet school in Chicago, had seven military recruiter visits last year, compared to 150 from university recruiters; Schurz High School, 80% Hispanic, had nine military and 10 university visits.

Bob Herbert, in the June 16, 2005, *New York Times*, notes that all high schools are not equal to recruiters: "Schools with kids from wealthier families (and a high percentage of college-bound students) are not viewed as good prospects. . . . The kids in those schools are not the kids who fight America's wars." Absent arts and sports programs or a generous array of clubs and activities, JROTC and its accompanying culture of war—militarism, aggression, violence, repression, the demonization of others, and mindless obedience—become the default choice for poor kids attending low-income schools.

The military culture seeps in at all levels and has a more generally corrosive impact on education itself, narrowing curriculum choices and promoting a model of teaching as training and of learning as "just following orders." In reality, good teaching always involves thoughtful and complicated judgments, careful attention to relationships, and complex choices about how to challenge and nurture each student.

Good teachers are not drill instructors. Authentic learning, too, is multidimensional and requires the constant construction and reconstruction of knowledge built on expanding experiences.

The educational model that employs teachers to simply pour imperial gallons of facts into empty vessels—ridiculed by Charles Dickens 150 years ago and discredited as a path to learning by modern psychologists and educational researchers—is making a roaring comeback. The rise of the military in schools adds energy to that.

A vibrant democratic culture requires free people with minds of their own capable of making independent judgments. Education in a democracy resists obedience and conformity for free inquiry and the widest possible exploration. Obedience training may have a place in instructing dogs, but not in educating citizens.

Keeping the Numbers Up

Today, two years into the invasion of Iraq [in 2003], recruiters are consistently failing to meet monthly enlistment quotas, despite deep penetration into high schools, sponsorship of NASCAR and other sporting events, and a $3 billion Pentagon recruitment budget. Recruiters are offering higher bonuses and shortened tours of duty, and violations of ethical guidelines and the military's own putative standards are becoming commonplace: In one highly publicized case, a recruiter was taped coaching a high school kid how to fake a mandatory drug test.

"One of the most common lies told by recruiters," writes Dobie, "is that it's easy to get out of the military if you change your mind. But once they arrive at training, the recruits are told there's no exit period." Although recruiters are known to lie, the number of young people signing up is still plummeting.

The military manpower crisis includes escalating desertions: 4,739 Army deserters in 2001 compared to 1,509 in 1995. An Army study says deserters tend to be "Younger when they enlist, less educated . . . come from 'broken homes,' and [have] 'engaged in delinquent behavior.'"

In war time, desertion tends to spike upward. So, after 9/11, the Army "issued a new policy regarding deserters, hoping to staunch the flow." The new rules return deserters to their units, hoping they can be "integrated back into the ranks"—not a happy circumstance: "I can't afford to babysit problem children everyday," says one commander.

At the end of March 2005, the Pentagon announced the active-duty Army achieved only about two-thirds of its March goal and was 3,973 short for the year; Army Reserve was 1,382 short of its year-to-date goal. 2005 was the toughest recruiting year since 1973, the first year of the all-volunteer Army. Americans don't want to fight this war, and a huge investment in high school recruiting is the military's latest desperate hope.

The Home Front

The high school itself has become a battlefield for hearts and minds. On one side: the power of the federal government; claims (often unsubstantiated) of financial benefits; humvees on school grounds; goody bags filled with donuts, key chains, video games, and T-shirts. Most ominous of all is No Child Left Behind, the controversial omnibus education bill of 2001.

Its Section 9528 reverses policies in many cities keeping organizations that discriminate on the basis of race, gender, or sexual orientation—including the military—out of schools. It mandates that military recruiters have the same access to students as colleges. The bill also requires schools to turn over students' addresses and home phone numbers to the military unless parents expressly opt out.

On the other side: a mounting death toll in Iraq, a growing sense among the citizenry that politicians lied and manipulated us at every turn to wage an aggressive war outside any broad popular interest, and groups of parents mobilizing to oppose high school recruitment.

A front-page story in the *New York Times* reported a "Growing Problem for Military Recruiters: Parents." Resistance to recruiters, says the report, is spreading coast to coast, and "was provoked by the very law that was supposed to make it easier for recruiters to reach students more directly. 'No Child Left Behind' . . . is often the spark that ignites parental resistance."

The military injunction—hierarchy, obedience, conformity, and aggression—stands in stark opposition to the democratic imperative of respect, cooperation, and equality.

And parents, it turns out, can be a formidable obstacle to a volunteer Army. Unlike the universal draft, signing up requires an affirmative act, and parents can and often do exercise a strong negative drag on their kids' stepping forward. A Department of Defense survey from November 2004 found that "only 25% of parents would recommend military service to their children, down from 42% in August 2003."

Herbert focuses attention on an Army publication called "School Recruiting Program Handbook." Its goal is straightforward: "school ownership that can only lead to a greater number of Army enlistments." This means promoting military participation in every feasible dimension, from making classroom presentations to involvement in Hispanic heritage and Black History months.

The handbook recommends that recruiters contact athletic coaches and volunteer to lead calisthenics, get involved with the homecoming committee and organize a presence in the parade, donate coffee and donuts to the faculty on a regular basis, eat in the cafeteria, and target influential students who, while they may not enlist, can refer others who might.

For Adults Only

The military injunction—hierarchy, obedience, conformity, and aggression—stands in stark opposition to the democratic imperative of respect, cooperation, and equality. The noted New Zealand educator Sylvia Ashton-Warner wrote that war and peace—acknowledged or hidden—"wait and vie" in every classroom.

She argued that all human beings are like volcanoes with two vents, one destructive and the other creative. If the creative vent is open, she maintained, then the destructive vent will atrophy and close; on the other hand, if the creative vent is shut down, the destructive will have free rein.

"Creativity in this time of life," she wrote, "when character can be influenced forever, is the solution to the problem of war." She quoted Erich Fromm: "The amount of destructiveness in a child is proportionate to the amount to which the expansiveness of his life has been curtailed. Destructiveness is the outcome of the unlived life."

Herbert, himself a Vietnam combat vet, is deeply troubled by the deceptive and manipulative tactics of recruiters: "Let the Army be honest and upfront in its recruitment," he writes. "War is not child's play, and warriors shouldn't be assembled through the use of seductive sales pitches to youngsters too immature to make an informed decision on matters that might well result in them having to kill others, or being killed themselves."

A little truth-telling, then. War is catastrophic for human beings, and, indeed, for the continuation of life on Earth. With 120 military bases around the globe and the second largest military force ever assembled, the U.S. government is engaged in a constant state of war, and American society is necessarily distorted and disfigured around the aims of war. . . .

Youth Warriors

There are now more than 300,000 child soldiers worldwide. . . .

The United States, which consistently refused to ratify the United Nations Convention on the Rights of the Child, agreed in 2002 to sign on to the "Optional Protocol" to the Convention, covering the involvement of children in armed conflicts. In its "Declarations and Reservations," the U.S. stipulated that the Protocol in no way carries any obligations under the Convention and that "nothing in the Protocol establishes a basis for jurisdiction by any international tribunal, including the International Criminal Court."

It lists several other reservations, including an objection to Article 1 of the Protocol, which states, "Parties shall take all feasible measures to ensure that members of their armed forces who have not attained the age of 18 years do not take direct part in hostilities."

Timely Advice

The U.S. stipulates that "feasible measures" means what is "practical" when taking into account all circumstances, "including humanitarian and military considerations," and that the article does not apply to "indirect participation in hostilities, such as gathering and transmitting military information, transporting weapons, ammunition, or other supplies, or forward deployment."

Because recruiters do lie, because the U.S. steps back from international law and standards, and because the cost of an education for too many poor and working-class kids is constructed as a trip through a minefield and a pact with the devil, teachers should consider Bill Bigelow's advice to critically examine the "Enlistment/Reenlistment Document—Armed Forces of the United States" that recruits sign when they join up. (Copies can be downloaded at rethinking schools.org.)

Among a host of loopholes and disclaimers is this in section 9b: "Laws and regulations that govern military personnel may change without notice to me. Such changes may affect my status, pay, allowances, benefits, and responsibilities as a member of the armed forces regardless of the provisions of this enlistment/reenlistment document."

When Bigelow's students analyzed the entire contract, they concluded it more honest to simply say something like, "Just sign up. . . . Now you belong to us." They advise students; "Read the contract thoroughly. . . . Don't sign unless you're 100% sure, 100% of the time." One of Bigelow's students, who had suffered through the war in Bosnia, recommended students inclined to enlist might "shoot a bird, and then think about whether you can kill a human."

Jermaine Lewis, the 23-year-old vet from Chicago who spoke of the war being "bogus" in Purple Hearts, always wanted to be a teacher but worried about the low pay. Now, with both legs gone, he calculates that a teacher's salary plus disability pay will earn him an adequate income: "So I want to go to college and study education—public school, primarily middle school, sixth to eighth grade." He went through the minefield to get what more privileged kids have access to without asking. It's something.

2

Bad Military Recruiters Are the Exception and Not the Rule

Rod Powers

Rod Powers is a retired U.S. Air Force First Sergeant, public speaker, and military author. His Barron's Guide to Officer Candidate School Tests *was released for publication in October 2006.*

The vast majority of recruiters are hard-working and honest professionals whose reputations can be hurt by the few "bad apples" that can be found in any profession, including the military. The job of a military recruiter is to find a sufficient number of qualified volunteers to fill projected vacancies for the fiscal year. The recruiting system is set up as a numbers game and it is true that recruiters are often judged by their superiors according to the number of recruits signed up. When recruiters stretch the truth, or when prospective recruits selectively listen to answers to their questions, everyone loses.

The vast majority of U.S. Military recruiters are honest, hard-working professionals, completely dedicated to the core values of their service. In fact, few military personnel put in more hours of work per week than recruiters.

The recruiter's job is to find enough qualified volunteers to fill projected vacancies for the fiscal year, for their particular branch of service. While a majority of military recruiters

Rod Powers, "What the Recruiter Never Told You," *Your Guide to the U.S. Military*, 2007. © 2006 About, Inc., A part of The New York Times Company. All rights reserved. Reproduced by permission.

are hard-working, honest, and dedicated, there are some (and I emphasize *some*) recruiters who are tempted to bend the truth, and/or downright lie, and/or blatantly cheat in order to sign up a recruit. It happens often enough where we've all heard "horror stories" about military recruiters.

So, why do some recruiters do this?

It's because of the way the recruiting system is set up. It's a numbers game, pure and simple. Recruiters are judged by their superiors primarily upon the number of recruits they get to sign up. Sign up large numbers, and you're judged to be a good recruiter. Fail to sign up the minimum number assigned to you (known as "making mission"), and you can find your career at a dead-end. This policy pressures *some* recruiters to adopt unethical practices in order to "make mission."

Preventive Measures

So, you ask, "why don't the services put a stop to this?" Easier said, than done. Each of the services has recruiting regulations which make it a crime for recruiters to lie, cheat, or knowingly process applicants that they know are ineligible for enlistment. Recruiters are punished when they are caught violating the standards. However, the key phrase is "when they are caught." Not that easy to do, as there are usually no witnesses. It becomes a "he said/he said" type of deal.

I should also mention here that, in many cases, "lies" told by a recruiter are actually cases of selected listening by recruits. A recruiter may say, "Many of our bases now have single rooms for most people," and the applicant may hear, "You are definitely not going to have a roommate." . . .

As I've said, most recruiters are honest. [My intent] is not to run down military recruiters, but rather inform potential recruits the truth about joining the military; the benefits and disadvantages of joining the military, whether for a four-year enlistment, or a 30-year military career. . . . I spent 23 years in the Air Force and enjoyed every minute of it. My primary profession today is to research/write about the United States Military. Both of my daughters are happily serving in the Air Force (one on active duty, one in the Air National Guard). I love the military and every aspect of it. . . .

Vision vs. Reality

However, the military is not for everyone. Fully 40 percent of recruits who enlist in the military today will not complete their full term of service. While many discharges will be for reasons beyond the recruit's control, such as medical problems that develop after joining the military, as a First Sergeant for 11 years, I found that a significant number of the *involuntary discharges* we imposed on first-term recruits was because they simply stopped trying—they discovered that the military wasn't what they thought it was going to be. Many of them told me that the military wasn't even close to what their recruiters told them it was going to be (either the recruiter lied to them, or they were guilty of "selective listening.") When this happens, everyone loses.

3

Military Recruiters Should Not Have Access to Students' Contact Information

Leah C. Wells

Leah C. Wells is the peace education coordinator for the Nuclear Peace Foundation.

The No Child Left Behind Act opened the door for military recruiters to gain unimpeded access to students' names, addresses, and telephone numbers, making it easy for them to contact youth at home. Combined with the presence of recruiters in schools, this can reinforce the perception that the military is the only option for students who don't succeed academically. But schools should be havens for higher learning, and not fertile fields of students ripe for the picking by military recruiters. The No Child Left Behind Act should serve as a wake-up call for all students to reclaim their privacy and demand more quality in educational rather than in military pursuits.

The No Child Left Behind Act which went into effect last week has some surprising implications for high school students. Buried deep within the funding benefits is Section 9528 which grants the Pentagon access to directories with students' names, addresses and phone numbers so that they may be more easily contacted and recruited for military service. Prior to this provision, one-third of the nation's high schools refused recruiters' requests for students' names or access to campus because they believed it was inappropriate for educational institutions to promote military service.

Leah C. Wells, "No Child Left Alone by Military Recruiters," *Humanist*, vol. 63, March–April 2003. Reproduced by permission of the author.

This portion of the Department of Education's initiative to create better readers, testers and homework-doers is a departure from the previously federally guaranteed privacy protections students have traditionally known. Until now, schools have been explicitly instructed to protect the integrity of students' information—even to guard students' private information from college recruiters. Students must consent to releasing their personal data when they take college entrance exams.

However, since September 11, 2001, educational institutions have slid down the slippery slope in doling out student information when solicited by the FBI and now the Pentagon. Only one university—Earlham in Richmond, Indiana—declined to release student data when approached after the terrorist attacks in the fall of 2001.

Checkpointing Access

The No Child Left Behind Act paves the way for the military to have unimpeded access to underage students who are ripe for solicitation for the military. This blatant contradiction of prior federal law is not only an invasion of students' privacy but an assault on their educational opportunities as well. Too many students are lulled by the siren songs of military service cooing promises of funding for higher education. Too many students have fallen between the cracks due to underfunded educational programs, underresourced schools and underpaid teachers. Such students penalized in their educational opportunities for the systemic failure to put our money where our priorities ought to be: in schools.

It is critical that students, schools and school districts have accurate information regarding this No Child Left Behind Act in preparation for the forthcoming military solicitation. First, the Local Educational Agency (LEA), not individual schools, may grant dissemination of student information. When recruiters approach individual schools, the administration should refer them to the school district office where they are supposed to visit in the first place.

In some cases, the recruiters on site have coerced employees at individual schools to sign previously prepared documents stating that in refusing to release student information, they are out of compliance with the No Child Left Behind Act and risk losing federal funding. All requests for student information should be referred to the school district's office and not left to the discretion of individual school employees. School boards, Parent-Teacher Organizations and Student Council/ASB groups can mobilize to support the administrations who are not willing to distribute private student information.

Second, students or their parents may opt themselves out of this recruitment campaign. So as not to be in violation of the previous federal law which restricts disclosure of student information, the LEA must notify parents of the change in federal policy through an addendum to the student handbook or individual letters sent to students' homes. Parents and students can notify their school administration and district in writing of their desire to have their records kept private.

At the heart of this argument over students' records and privacy is the true purpose and meaning of education.

The San Francisco School District has maintained a policy of non-recruitment by the military and is leading the nation in their efforts to educate parents and students on their right to privacy. As advocates for their students, the district is sending home individual letters to parents outlining their options for protecting their child's information.

Education vs. Solicitation

At the heart of this argument over students' records and privacy is the true purpose and meaning of education. Is the goal of education to provide a fertile field of students ripe for the picking by the military which will send them to the front lines of battle, potentially never to return? Is the essence of education to dichotomize the availability of quality education between those with ample finances and those with no financial mobility?

Students are continually guilted into shouldering the burden of responsibility when they do not succeed in school and all too often accept as inevitable their fate of being sucked into military service.

Or is education meant to develop students' minds, hearts and talents through self-discovery and academic exploration? Does education aim to promote critical thinking skills, empathy for others, understanding of individual roles in community service, and a sense of global connectedness? Was education designed to be an equitable opportunity for all students?

A newspaper from the U.K., *The Scotsman*, recently interviewed a young American woman on an aircraft carrier in the Middle East. Eighteen-year-old Karen de la Rosa said, "I have no idea what is happening. I just hear the planes launching above my head and pray that no one is going to get killed. I keep telling myself I'm serving my country."

But is her country serving her?

The relationship between militarism and education is evident. The current Department of Education budget proposal for 2003 is $56.5 billion. The recently approved Department of Defense budget is $396 billion—nearly seven times what is allocated for education, and more than three times the combined military budgets of Russia, China, Iraq, Iran, North Korea, Libya, Cuba, Sudan and Syria. An escalated war in Iraq [fighting in Iraq began in March 2003, after this article was written] could add more than $200 billion to the defense budget as well.

Students are continually guilted into shouldering the burden of responsibility when they do not succeed in school and all too often accept as inevitable their fate of being sucked into military service. The Leave No Child Behind Act is a wake up call to students to reclaim their privacy, to reinvest their energy into demanding quality education and to remind their leaders that stealing money from education to pay for military is unacceptable.

4

Military Recruiting Exploits the Vulnerability of Teens

Terry J. Allen

Terry J. Allen is a senior editor of In These Times, *a magazine dedicated to informing and analyzing popular movements for social, environmental and economic justice. Her work has appeared in* Harper's, The Nation, New Scientist, *and elsewhere.*

The United States military markets itself to children as young as thirteen. This marketing exploits American youth because they are physically incapable of making such important on-the-spot decisions about their futures. The teenage brain has an underdeveloped impulse control; thus, teens may be easily swayed into joining the military by persistent recruiters, without really giving their decision serious thought. Some recruiters' aggressive tactics further exploit teens by making them or their parents think that military service is mandatory, or by otherwise tricking them into signing enlistment papers.

Almost 600,000 of America's 1 million active and reserve soldiers enlisted as teens. The military lures these physiologically immature kids with a PR machine that would make Joe Camel proud.

While the age of legal and cultural adulthood can vary, science is now able to determine the physiological markers of maturity. A recent study headed by Jay Giedd of the National Institutes of Health using MRI scans shows that the brain of

Terry J. Allen, "Pentagon's Teen Recruiting Methods Would Make Tobacco Companies Proud," www.alternet.org, May 22, 2007. Reproduced by permission of the publsiher, www.inthesetimes.com.

an 18-year-old is not fully developed, with the limbic cortex-brain structures, the cerebellum and prefrontal cortex still undergoing substantial changes.

As of March 31 [2007] the U.S. military included 81,000 teenagers. Its 7,350 17-year-olds needed parental consent to enlist, and only this April were all barred from battle zones.

But the military aims even lower, marketing itself to children as young as 13 with multimedia videos, school visits and cold calls to teens' homes and cell phones. In Junior ROTC, kids get uniforms, win medals, fire real guns and play soldier, while adults trained in psychological manipulation steer them toward the army. The Army's JROTC website lists such motivating activities as "eating at concession stands."

Teens Are Not Mature Enough to Decide to Enlist

A mature prefrontal cortex, "the area of sober second thought," is vital not only to deciding whether to enlist, but also to choices made under the stress of deployment and the terrors of combat. But the prefrontal cortex, "important for controlling impulses, is among the last brain regions to mature," according to Giedd, and doesn't reach "adult dimensions until the early 20s."

Teenagers' brains simply lack the impulse control that can prevent a lifetime of regret, psychological and physical disability, and preventable deaths—their own, their fellow soldiers' and those of civilians.

The child soldier problem is global and so is America's part in it. More than 300,000 children around the world, some as young as seven, serve as soldiers, or, in the case of girls, as military sex slaves. The State Department reports that 10 countries are violating international treaties against child soldiers. Washington provides military assistance to nine of these outlaw nations: Afghanistan, Burundi, Chad, Colombia, Ivory Coast, Democratic Republic of Congo, Sri Lanka, Sudan and Uganda.

The reason the United States and other militaries target children is their need for cannon fodder, coupled with the vulnerability of youth. In 2002, almost half of Marine recruits were 17 or 18. A Pentagon survey found that "for both males and females, propensity [to enlist] is highest among 16- and 17-year-olds." That "propensity" quickly declines with age.

A 2004 Pentagon database listed the number of 16- and 17-year-olds who applied for active service enlistment at 69,000 and 18-year-olds at 73,000. By 19, the count had dropped to 49,000 and by age 24 had plummeted to 9,700.

The Department of Defense (DoD) spends more than $4 billion a year on recruiting with $1.5 billion for advertising and maintaining the recruiting stations staffed by more than 22,000 recruiters. Much of that money goes to convincing children to become soldiers.

Aggressive Tactics Exploit Teens

A recruiters handbook discusses creepy seduction techniques with all the subtlety of predatory stalking. Adult recruiters skilled in "projecting credibility" lurk in snack joints, set up laptops playing action-packed videos, proffer rides and promise friendship and fatherly advice. With blacks particularly skeptical of the war effort, the military is aggressively targeting Hispanics with multimillion dollar marketing campaigns that include chatting up mothers and attending church. Recruiters get non-English speaking parents to sign enlistment papers for 17-year-olds by letting them believe that service is mandatory, or that they were approving blood tests, according to the *New York Times*.

Recruiters also try to win over high school guidance counselors with offers of "extended tours, VIP trips ('A day in the life of a sailor') or workshops."

A DoD training manual instructs recruiters to appropriate the techniques that pharmaceutical salespeople use to convince doctors to prescribe the most profitable drugs: "Pharmaceutical representatives court doctors and provide incentives to them in exchange for listening to a sales pitch and considering their products." DoD advises following the pharma model by offering "personalized incentives in exchange for some of their time (bring food when asking favors.)"

The manual suggests bribing teachers: "Provide lunch for teachers in exchange for information." It quotes an anonymous teacher: "Giving teachers pencils and calendars lets us know that you understand our needs and support us. We, in turn, are more likely to support your efforts in the future."

"Chiefs of warfare reach out to children precisely because they are innocent, malleable, impressionable," says Olara Otunnu, the U.N. Special Representative for Children and Armed Conflict.

The science is clear: Turning children below the age of brain maturity into soldiers, whether in the United States or Sudan, exploits that vulnerability.

5

Military Recruiters Can Provide Youths Many Options Besides Combat

Jorge Correa

Jorge Correa is a staff writer for the Pasadena City College Courier online.

If students will not listen to what recruiters have to say, they will never know of some great programs and opportunities that could be beneficial to them. Just because someone enlists in the military to defend our country does not mean that he or she will be handed a gun and sent to the front lines. There is a need for everything from doctors and x-ray technicians to electronics experts, mechanics, and aviators. And there is no way to estimate the value of all the life experiences one might gain, including overseas travel and just learning how other people live. Young adults should keep an open mind, because a recruiter might just say something that sparks real interest.

It's too bad that knowledge is scant about what a brief military career can offer an individual. And it comes as no surprise when recruiters on campus get completely shunned by the very students they hope to enlist. No one wants to go to Iraq and die, and that seems to be the general argument against joining the military.

Without even making eye contact, one student walked straight past a recruiter and said, "Sorry, I don't feel like dying."

Jorge Correa, "Military Recruiters Offer Real Benefits," *The Pasadena City College Courier*, December 7, 2006. © 2006, Courier. All rights reserved. Reproduced by permission.

Business major Ko Nishimoto said, "I'll talk to them when they stop me, but I have no desire to join. I'm 26 now and that option has diminished. I don't want to be gone for four years then start school again when I'm 30."

PCC [Pasadena City College] student Sophia Kritselis believes if someone wants to join the military then they should seek them out. "I don't believe they should come to campus or try recruiting people at the mall. If people want to join, then go to them."

There are hundreds of different jobs within each branch to choose from, along with programs that will help you in your education and career.

With four branches to choose from, five if you count the Coast Guard, each one has special programs and opportunities that could be beneficial to students at PCC. But they will never know if they don't take the time to at least hear what recruiters have to say.

I know there are some students who have worked hard for scholarships and grants or some other form of financial aid and have the next four-to-six years planned out. But what about those who don't?

Just because you decide to enlist in the military and defend your country, that doesn't mean you're going to get handed an M-16 and then get sent straight to the frontlines. There are hundreds of different jobs within each branch to choose from, along with programs that will help you in your education and career.

I spent five years working with Navy aircraft, such as the F-18 Super Hornet, the F-14 Tomcat Fighter and MH-60 Night Hawk helicopter. My favorite job was when I was attached to a search and rescue helicopter squadron in Guam and served as a flight deck landing signalman.

I was in the aviation field, but recruits may choose from electronics, administration, medical and more. For example, PCC has a great nursing program, and once equipped with a degree, a graduate can join the military as an officer and work in a base hospital.

It's not just nurses. There's a need for everything from doctors, x-ray technicians, pharmacists and optometrists to man base medical facilities. There are also opportunities in every aspect of dentistry as well.

The most popular program is the Montgomery GI Bill, which is offered by each branch. By giving up $100 a month out of my paycheck for only the first year I served, it has now turned into roughly $36,000 for school.

According to PCC's veterans affair office, our campus currently has just over 300 students who are currently collecting veterans benefits. Sure I did a full five years before I started collecting money, but that doesn't have to be the case. Many active duty personnel now collect their GI Bill money while they are serving.

Where else can you shoot 18 holes of golf on a tropical island that just happens to be in your own backyard, every day before or after work?

Depending on the number of units you have, you can enlist at a higher rank than someone who doesn't have any. I joined as an E-1, the lowest pay grade, and with good conduct it took me nine months to get the next rank. If I had over 60 units, I could have jumped two pay grades and started as an E-3 right away. And do you know what comes with higher rank? A higher pay check.

Besides the GI Bill, each branch offers forms of educational benefits of their own as well. For instance the Army has the Army College Fund which adds more money to the GI Bill, making it worth up to $50,000. The Navy has PACE or

Programs Afloat for a College Education, which allow sailors to earn degrees while aboard a ship. Trust me, I wish I would of done that with my spare time on the ship, instead of becoming a master at Halo.

Although each branch is similar in ways, choosing a branch to enlist in can be difficult, and like most decisions, you have to weigh the ups and downs that are personal to you. The small spaces, long hours, and separation from family and friends for months at a time were not easy to endure. Ship life was hard.

Some branches invest their money in areas that others don't. For example, Air Force recruiter Staff Sergeant Derek Hudson said, "The Army likes to put a lot of their money into advertisement, where the Air Force puts the money into their people. We have a better quality of life."

For instance, Air Force bases are first-rate with more amenities. Although I was Navy enlisted, in Guam I was stationed on Anderson Air Force Base, and this was where I learned to golf. Where else can you shoot 18 holes on a tropical island that just happens to be in your own backyard, every day before or after work?

Also, Air Force barracks are in better shape. I had my own mock-studio apartment, with a full kitchen and my own bathroom. Food on the Air Force base was better too. I would put Anderson's galley food up against Fresno State's dorm food any time.

Bottom line, I would do it again if I had to, in order to be where I am today. Plus, you can't put a price on all the life experiences, like traveling overseas and visiting exotic foreign places. Whether it's attending college, being in the labor force or joining the military, it's what you make of it that counts. So keep in mind that one of these recruiters might say something that sparks your interest.

6

Concerned Citizens Should Take Action Against Military Recruiting in Schools

Ron Jacobs

Ron Jacobs is the author of two books and a regular contributing essayist to the online publication, www.counterpunch.org.

The military is becoming increasingly intrusive in its attempts to recruit college and high school students, using the Solomon Amendment to force schools to provide personal information about students and allow recruiting even if it goes against school policy. Anti-war and anti-recruitment activists have responded in a variety of ways, including petitions, protests, opting out, and lawsuits. These efforts should continue. In addition, the anti-recruitment effort should broaden its campaign to include opposition to defense contractors and others who benefit from war, and by examining the very role of the military.

Recently, most students at the University of Vermont (UVM) in Burlington received an email with the heading ARMY PAYS OFF STUDENT LOANS in their university email box. The general message of the mass mailing was that if a student was nearing graduation and wondering how they were going to pay off the massive debt today's U.S. college students incur, they should join the army. In essence, this email was a college student's version of the poverty draft that entraps so many working class and poor young people into enlisting in

Ron Jacobs, "Let The Pentagon Pay Off Those Loans, Lies Military Recruiters Tell," *CounterPunch*, Weekend Edition, March 5–6, 2005. Reproduced by permission.

the service. The sender was a military recruiter working out of the U.S. Army recruitment office in the Burlington suburb of Williston. Given that the university has a very clear policy forbidding these types of solicitations on their email servers one wonders how the recruiting office was able to obtain the address list. The university administration has been reticent when asked this question by various faculty, students, and parents. It is fair to assume, however, that the email list was released to the recruiter under the compliance sections of the so-called Solomon Amendment. For those unfamiliar with this legislation, it essentially forbids Department of Defense (DOD) funding of schools unless those schools provide military representatives access to their students for recruiting purposes. It is this same law that enables military recruiters to set up shop in high schools across the U.S. and to call students at their homes attempting to entice them into joining the military.

[I]n high schools across the U.S., more students and their parents seem to be opting out of taking the Armed Services Vocational Aptitude Battery (ASVAB), a test given to high school juniors as a method of targeting potential recruits.

At UVM, this email was met with anger and questions, and probably even a few inquiries. The anger is now being organized into a drive to keep military recruiters off the university campus and out of the students' private communications. There is a petition campaign underway that demands that no recruiters for the regular military or the Vermont National Guard be allowed to recruit on campus. Despite this, recruiters do show up unannounced on campus. One assumes that their strategy is designed to prevent student organizers from organizing protests against the recruiters' presence. In addition, there is organizing underway to organize some kind of response to the military and Guard's presence at the University's Spring Career Day on March 8th. (This career day is also the host to recruiters from various corporations from the war industry—General Dynamics foremost among them). Here in Vermont, the Guard recruitment hits close to home, since the state ranks near the top in the number of deaths per capita in Iraq. The likelihood of the university denying these recruiters access is slim, especially in light of the mass email, yet the students involved continue on undaunted. If the petition campaign fails to produce the results they desire, there will likely be some kind of protest.

Other college campuses have already experienced such protests. On January 20, 2005, several hundred students at Seattle Central Community College chased army recruiters from their spot in the Student center. On February 23, campus police arrested a woman student during a picket in front of the military's recruitment table at a job fair at the University of Wisconsin-Madison. A couple days before that, several dozen students chased military recruiters off campus at Southern Connecticut State University (SCSU). In September 2004, more than a hundred students protested the presence of military recruiters at the University of Pennsylvania. On February 22, 2005 several dozen students picketed recruiters at the University of Illinois campus in Chicago. At the USC Law School, recruiters were met with pickets and leafleters demanding that they leave, and at UC Berkeley, a couple dozen students protested the presence of a military recruiter table there. These are but a few of the dozens of protests that have taken place.

Meanwhile, in high schools across the U.S., more students and their parents seem to be opting out of taking the Armed Services Vocational Aptitude Battery (ASVAB), a test given to high school juniors as a method of targeting potential recruits. It is an admissions and placement test for the U.S. military. All persons enlisting in the U.S. military are required to take the ASVAB. Although the military does not usually start turning up the pressure to join the military until students reach their senior year, about 14,000 high schools nationwide give this test to juniors. A recent piece in the *Boston Globe* detailed the troubles one recruiting office in New Hampshire is facing this year. According to ASVAB testing coordinator at the Military Entrance Processing Station in Boston, which handles enlistment processing for Rhode Island, much of New Hampshire and parts of Massachusetts, many parents are writing notes excusing their kids from taking the test. At one high school in Nashua, NH, school administrators opted out of even administering the test this year. This is not an isolated case either; of the thirty schools in the Boston region that administered the test in 2004, only nineteen signed up to do so this year. One wonders how long it will be before the military makes the test mandatory for graduation.

In my mind, the best political strategy is one that challenges the imperial policies of the U.S. and calls into question not just the military's discriminatory recruitment policies, but also the role of the military itself.

Campus antiwar groups that formed in the past three years have called most of the university and college protests. In addition, lesbian and gay organizations and individuals have joined in because of their opposition to the military's "don't ask, don't tell" policy on homosexuality. Of course, many of the latter group also oppose the war in Iraq. According to a federal appeals court ruling made in November 2004, the essentially anti-gay policies of the military do allow universities to deny its recruiters access to their students and property. On top of that ruling, another federal judge in Connecticut found that the government unconstitutionally applied the Solomon Amendment after Yale Law School faculty sued Donald Rumsfeld when he attempted to deny federal funds to Yale because it prevented military recruitment on its campus.

Yale denied the recruiters access because of their discriminatory policies against gays and lesbians.

While this strategy is not necessarily the best political strategy possible to chase recruiters off campus, it is a legal tool counter-recruitment activists should utilize while it exists. In my mind, the best political strategy is one that challenges the imperial policies of the U.S. and calls into question not just the military's discriminatory recruitment policies, but also the role of the military itself. A strategy based on this premise would not only diminish the military's visibility, it would also challenge young people (and the rest of us) to examine for whom and what the military really fights. Additionally, it would allow the organizers of these campaigns to include defense contractors in their campaign. After all, it is these corporations that truly need young men and women to go to war.

7

Colleges Should Not Deny Access to Military Recruiters

Debra Saunders

In FAIR v. Rumsfeld, 126 S.Ct. 1297 (2006), the U.S. Supreme Court unanimously rejected the collective argument of several law schools that they were justified in denying campus access to military recruiters because of the military's anti-gay discrimination policy. The Court basically said if universities cannot accept the "don't ask, don't tell" policy, they are free to reject federal funds for their schools. The academic world has argued that it is hypocrisy to preach against discrimination while allowing recruiters to discriminate against gays. Saunders argues that it is academia that is hypocritical. In a truly free academic environment, students would accept the presence of persons and ideologies different than their own, and respect others' right to express opposing views. This allows the students to choose their associations themselves, as it should be.

Law schools that challenged the Solomon Amendment, a federal law passed in 1994 that eliminates federal funding to universities that deny equal access to military recruiters, tried to hide behind noble motives. The Forum for Academic and Institutional Rights, for example, claimed that its support of academic freedom and nondiscrimination required law schools to bar military recruiters from campus because of the military's discriminatory "don't ask, don't tell" policy on gays.

This week [March 2006], the U.S. Supreme Court rejected the lawsuit unanimously. As the opinion written by Chief Jus-

Debra Saunders, "The Wisdom of Solomon," *San Francisco Chronicle*, March 9, 2006, p. B9. © Hearst Communications, Inc. All rights reserved. Republished with permission of San Francisco Chronicle, conveyed through Copyright Clearance Center, Inc.

tice John Roberts noted, the Solomon Amendment doesn't, in any way, limit universities' rights to protest "don't ask, don't tell." If universities cannot abide by the policy, Roberts wrote, they are "free to decline the federal funds."

But you see, this lawsuit was all about letting academia have it both ways. Clearly the law-school litigants believe they have a constitutional right to thumb their nose at military policies, while burning through tax dollars paid by voters who, as a rule, hold those who serve in the military in high esteem—and no doubt respect soldiers more than they respect lawyers.

It's so, well, lawyer-like for academics to argue that they have deeply-held convictions—but that doesn't mean they should have to pay any consequences for them.

Besides, where is the academic freedom in barring recruiters from campus? Freedom should mean that military recruiters have their platform. Students are free to enlist, if they so choose, or not enlist if they do not. Critics are free to protest against Pentagon practices. It's called a free exchange of ideas.

(This may be a good place to mention, I think "don't ask, don't tell" is a foolish policy. I think the military should welcome gays, that it is wrong-headed to assume gay officers will misbehave, and that existing rules can address any wrongful actions of any gay or straight officers.)

In barring the military, law students and faculty are working to marginalize not only recruits, but also any students who support military policy.

Think about it. If the Bushies wanted to bar Muslim recruiting on campus, academics would be hollering—despite Islam's hostility toward homosexuality. The big dif here is that fellow academics have decided who cannot speak freely on campus.

Pentagon rules discriminate against women by barring all women from serving in certain combat positions. I wondered: If ivory-tower elites truly oppose discrimination, why didn't they challenge the Solomon Amendment on military policies that discriminate against all women?

Plaintiff Michael Rooke-Ley, a law prof at Santa Clara University, answered that military recruiters will interview females, but they won't interview gay students. I reply that the military will interview gay law students who don't announce that they are homosexual. Rooke-Ley believes no institution should expect applicants to deny a fundamental fact about themselves. You can't argue that it is acceptable to discriminate against Jews because someone can deny being Jewish, he said. The same goes for homosexuality.

Rooke-Ley sees the lawsuit as a way to fight "hypocrisy on campus"—that law schools can't preach against discrimination, then allow recruiters that discriminate.

I see the suit itself as the height of hypocrisy. In a truly free academic environment, students would accept the presence of those with whom they disagree, while exercising their right to speak against them. In barring the military, law students and faculty are working to marginalize not only recruits, but also any students who support military policy. It's not enough to protest recruiters. Only a solid ban will do to let students interested in military service understand that, in the university, they are the freaks.

They don't care that, to the extent that this is a free country, you can thank the military.

8

Recruiter Denial to College Campuses Would Harm Society and the Military

Sean Aqui

Sean Aqui is the pen name of a regular contributing writer for blogcritics.org. After graduating from college through the ROTC program, he served in the military as a second lieutenant in the armor branch.

The U.S. Supreme Court flatly rejected the free-speech challenge by several law schools that had banned military recruiters from campuses because of the military's policy on homosexuals. Notwithstanding, the schools' argument was not without merit. Why should military recruiters be exempt from discrimination rules that apply to other recruiters or companies that are allowed on campus? Further, allowing recruiters to discriminate against gays might create the appearance that a school might condone such a policy even if it is against the school's own policies. However, at the end of the day, fair is fair. Banning military recruiters from campuses goes too far. Too many bright and talented officers— 70 percent of whom receive their commissions through ROTC— would be lost. This would not only adversely affect national security, but also would further isolate the military from mainstream society. People can publicly protest or declare their support for gays in the military, but derailing the ROTC cripples not only the military, but all of us.

Sean Aqui, "Why Everyone Should Want Military Recruiters On Campus," *Blogcritics Online Magazine*, March 6, 2006. Reproduced by permission.

The Supreme Court has ruled [in *FAIR* v. Rumsfeld, 2006] that colleges that accept federal money must allow military recruiters on campus. The case involved some law schools who had banned the recruiters because the military's policy on homosexuals violates the schools' own policies.

The ruling was unanimous, so there's not a lot of room for interpretation: if you want federal money, military recruiters come with it.

FAIR Is Fair

I sympathize with the schools to some extent. There's a fairness issue: Why should the military be exempt from rules that apply to every other recruiter or company that has access to a given school? In addition, there's the appearance of condoning discrimination.

But I bring another perspective to the case, having been commissioned through ROTC and witnessed the same debate and protests while I was in college in the late 1980s at the University of Minnesota.

If military culture grows too separated from civilian culture we risk a 'Prussification' of the military—an insular society led by elites that have little in common with the people whom they ostensibly serve.

First, let me be clear: I think the military's policy on gays is asinine, the discrimination both unfounded and unnecessary. The military has plenty of rules on conduct and fraternization that would maintain discipline even if soldiers were openly gay, just as they manage to maintain discipline where heterosexual men and women serve alongside each other. And, in an era when the military is having difficulty meeting recruiting goals, turning away thousands of otherwise qualified (in some cases, highly qualified) soldiers makes no sense from a national-security standpoint.

Throwing Out the Baby With the Bathwater

The problem, as I see it, is one of relative weight. Military access to college campuses is simply too important to be derailed by the military's gay policy. Protest? Fine. Work to change minds? Fine. Declare and demonstrate support for military gays? Of course. But banning ROTC and recruiters goes too far, doing real damage to our security and further isolating the military from mainstream society.

When I was in the military, 70 percent of officers received their commissions through ROTC—including some of the brightest and best-educated soldiers. Simply put, that is an irreplaceable source of military leaders. If we ban ROTC and recruiters, we cripple the future of the military—and thus our security.

A second point that opponents should consider is somewhat subversive. Soldiers recruited from college campuses tend to have a broader education and life exposure than those who are educated in the hothouses of service academies and military schools. They bring that with them into the military, forming the main part of what might be considered the "liberal" wing of the military. They help ensure that mainstream American values continue to be represented in military culture.

This is crucial, coming as it does at a time when fewer and fewer people know someone who is in the military. If military culture grows too separated from civilian culture we risk a "Prussification" of the military—an insular society led by elites that have little in common with the people whom they ostensibly serve. That would be a disaster on many levels.

The military must be given access to college students both to maintain our physical security and to save the military from itself.

9

Counter-Recruitment Efforts Are Needed to Save Our Youths

Don Trent Jacobs

Don Trent Jacobs is an author and associate professor in the Educational Leadership Department at Northern Arizona University. He also serves on the faculty of the Educational Leadership and Change College at Fielding Graduate Institute.

Military recruiters are committing a fraud upon our youth. They are luring them into dangerous service in an immoral war with promises of benefits few will receive in full. They have the backing of the government, and an all-out draft could be next. It is up to parents and educators to inform America's youth and save them from the military.

Some think that because I was an officer in the U.S. Marine Corps during the Viet Nam War, I have a special right to challenge military recruitment in public schools. Not so. Every teacher, school administrator, and parent has this right. Moreover, I believe each has the responsibility to do so if and when the recruiting is fraudulent.

Actual Fraud

In law, fraud is understood as an intentional perversion of truth undertaken with the intent to induce another to part with some valuable thing. In this case, the valuable item is a

Don Trent Jacobs, "Reading, Writing, and Counter-Recruiting," *Paths of Learning*, vol. 22, Autumn 2004, pp. 29–30. Reproduced by permission.

teenager's life. The perversion has to do with lies about education and health benefits for veterans; about the value of military training for one's future; about the psychological and physical costs of war; and about the legal and moral issues relating to the rationale for a particular war.

For example, only 35% of veterans will receive any money for college and only 15% will earn a four-year degree. (The government makes more money from the $1200 it receives in the form of non-refundable payroll deductions for future education benefits than it gives out for schooling!) V.A. medical benefits are shockingly inadequate. As for the legality or morality of war, how many of our high-school students are aware of the gross deceptions that brought us into Afghanistan and Iraq?

Moreover, the fraud occurring in our schools with respect to students' joining the military is legislated. Both Section 9528 of the NCLB [No Child Left Behind] law and the National Defense Authorization Act make it mandatory for high schools to provide recruiters with monthly quotas of juniors' and seniors' names, home addresses, and records. Growing numbers of schools now have recruiters on campuses throughout each school day. (If this is not bad enough, JROTC [Junior Reserve Officer Training Corps] programs are increasing, and 2/3 of the cost is paid by the school district!) Yet teachers, counselors, administrators, and parents do very little to teach "the other side" to students. (Ironically, Michael Moore's new film about the Iraq war [*Fahrenheit 9/11*] has been rated "R" so that the same Americans who are subjected to recruitment fraud cannot even watch film footage of the war's truths without being accompanied by an adult. Perhaps even more ironically, Moore's film documents the deceptive tactics used by military recruiters intent on enticing youths to join the military.)

Protecting Our Youths

Although still too few, more and more parents, teachers, and counselors are engaging in counter-recruitment education. Federal district and appellate courts have repeatedly upheld Equal Access Laws that enable students to receive opposing points of view. In fact, if a school district discourages students from having access to this opposing view, the school can be held liable. (For a listing of ways to offer this information, from publishing it in school newspapers to inviting speakers from Veterans for Peace chapters, go to ⟨www.objector.org⟩.)

Hopefully, educators and parents will nonetheless use their critical thinking skills to help them understand the severity of the military recruitment/drafting situation now facing our youth.

In 2003, the government spent 2.7 billion dollars for military recruiting (including 4 million dollars for a U.S. Army-sponsored race car). To save on this expense, legislators have introduced legislation for a draft. Although this pending legislation is highly controversial some think it will pass by July 2005. . . . [I]n addition to parents', teachers', and counselors' engaging in rigorous counter-recruiting efforts NOW, it is essential that all high-school students immediately familiarize themselves with both the requirements for and the difficulties in applying for conscientious objector status. There is no place on draft registration forms to check and, once drafted, one has fewer than ten days to make a claim for conscientious objection. Affidavits, as well as letters from teachers and others that demonstrate moral, ethical, and religious beliefs that preclude killing others or going to war, must be prepared well in advance. Remember, students claiming to be opposed to war on political, sociological, philosophical or personal grounds will be denied C.O. [conscientious objector] status. In other words, the law says that critical thinking is not allowed. Rather, moral or ethical objections must be affiliated with your religious perspective, and only well established religious conviction is taken into account for conscientious objector status. Hopefully, educators and parents will nonetheless use their critical thinking skills to help them understand the severity of the military recruitment/drafting situation now facing our youth. With such an understanding, they can gain or strengthen the conviction that they will need to have and maintain in their valiant counter-recruiting efforts undertaken on behalf of our nation's youth.

10

The Real Motivation for Anti-Recruiting Efforts Is Hatred of the Military

Jamie Weinstein

Jamie Weinstein was an upperclassman in the College of Arts and Sciences at Cornell University when he wrote this article.

Those opposed to recruiting on college campuses often justify their actions by pointing to the military's discriminatory policies toward homosexuals. They may be right that these policies are unfair or counterproductive, but this is not the genuine reason they are trying to stop recruitment efforts. What really motivates anti-recruitment activists is a dislike of the military and opposition to U.S. actions in Iraq. If activists' concerns about discrimination were really their priority, they would be trying to change the military's policy towards homosexuals. Instead they use that issue as a pretext while attempting to force the military off of college campuses, and often use suspect methods in the process.

I guess I overestimated the movement to drive our military off campus. While it is true I believed the motivating force behind it was hatred for our troops, and not "discrimination," I thought that the shameful protesters would at least try to hide this. Evidently not.

Writing in *The Sun*, Professors Moncrieff Cochran and William Trochim, along with students Patrick Young '06 and Bekah Ward grad, revealed their true intentions in trying to

Jamie Weinstein, "The Campus Left's War on ROTC," *FrontPageMagazine*, April 5, 2005, www.frontpagemag.com. Reproduced by permission.

remove the military from the University. After placating the discrimination argument, they turned to their real gripe: the United States military itself. They wrote, "we oppose military recruiter's presence on campus because they are selling a career in killing."

Make no mistake, the discrimination argument is a canard [a fake]. This coalition of radical writers, along with their considerable following, hates our military and our soldiers not because of anything relating to discriminatory practices, but because they consider them killers. Having failed to stop the liberation of Iraq with their rallies and teach-ins, these anti-war radicals have turned to another front to attack the U.S. Armed Forces.

Backstage

Behind the calls of "Support Our Troops—Bring Them Home," lies the belief that the U.S. military is not generally a force of good in the world, but rather a negative one. In their mind, American G.I.'s do not stand for freedom and protecting America, but rather are drones helping further American "imperialism." I'm not pulling this out of thin air. The authors admitted it themselves: "These recruiters further U.S. imperialism. . . ."

Not surprisingly, within this movement there rests no respect for the sacrifices made on a daily basis or the bravery habitually exhibited by the men and women of our Armed Forces. Instead of appreciation, these radicals spout condemnation. Their heroes do not overthrow mass murderers and protect American values, they ransack ROTC offices and spout off silly chants.

So let's get it straight from the start. All this talk about the Solomon Amendment being "illegal"—which in my opinion is nonsense—is just talk. It is merely another front in a continuing battle against the U.S. military by the radical left.

This Much Granted

Truth be told, there are legitimate questions that can be raised about "Don't Ask, Don't Tell." Personally, I'm conflicted over whether it is the right policy. On one hand I understand that permitting homosexuals in the military may create an uncomfortable environment. There are reasons why men and women do not share barracks today, and it is the same reason—or at least a major part of the reason—for the reluctance to allow gays into the service.

If Donald Rumsfeld announced tomorrow that gays would now be allowed in the military, no questions asked, the movement to drive the military off campus would not fade away.

On the other hand, other functioning and active militaries such as Britain and Israel have incorporated homosexuals. Furthermore, I find it counterproductive to dismiss gay translators, especially those who are proficient in Arabic, at a time when there is such a dire need for such linguists. When nine gay linguists were dismissed in 2002, some proficient in Arabic, I questioned if there could be some modification to "Don't Ask, Don't Tell" to allow them to remain.

But this is a question that one should bring to Congress if they were serious about strengthening America and our military. If one felt that barring gays from the military was hurting American interests and the strength of our armed services at a time when we are engaged in a great war, presumably they wouldn't want to take actions to further weaken them, even if they felt it may be following a discriminatory policy. By trying to force ROTC and military recruiters off campus they would be doing just that.

Calling Their Bluff

So clearly, the protesters—at least most of them—aren't demanding that the U.S. military change its position on "Don't

Ask, Don't Tell" so that the U.S. army would be strengthened. If Donald Rumsfeld announced tomorrow that gays would now be allowed in the military, no questions asked, the movement to drive the military off campus would not fade away. It would just adapt. They would have to develop another pretext to fight military recruitment and ROTC training on campus. As I said, the primary motivation is not discrimination, but loathing of the American military itself.

The article by the radical anti-war activists goes on to describe how at a recent Cornell Career Fair, activists bombarded military recruiters, claiming they were interested in joining the military. After wasting the recruiters' time, they proceeded to tell them that they were gay and asked whether that would be a problem.

After getting the answer they expected, the anti-war radicals began filling out bias related reports against the recruiters on campus in the middle of the career fair. The radical coalition of writers described it as follows: "There was an air of excitement, people getting involved and hundreds of supportive passers-by."

While it seems that the protesters had fun playing their anti-war games and stymieing military recruiters from doing their job, it also sounds like some false reports may have been filed. From what I gathered in the article and heard around campus, it sounded like non-gay activists also participated in the childish shenanigans and filed bias-related incident reports. If in fact this is true, and I would be willing to bet that it is, in filing the reports the non-gay students would be submitting reports to the Cornell administration that were false. You can't be discriminated against for being gay if you are not, in fact, gay.

After doing some research, it appears that such actions would violate Title III, Section II, Subsection C of the Campus Code of Conduct which states as a violation, "To furnish false information to the University with intent to deceive." The

Judicial Administrator should look into this to see if any false reports were filed, and if so, they should hold the offenders accountable.

11

The National Media Is Biased in Support of Anti-Recruitment Efforts

Warner Todd Huston

Warner Todd Huston is a widely-read columnist who is a regular contributor to many Web sites, including Renew America, Townhall, American Daily, *and* Opinion Editorials. *In addition to writing for several history magazines as well, Huston appears in the book,* Americans on Politics, Policy and Pop Culture.

The national news media goes out of its way to highlight problems with recruiting and gives free publicity to anti-recruitment efforts. It rarely presents the views of recruitment supporters.

With the talk of Charlie Rangel's [a U.S. Representative from New York] second try to get the draft reinstated, it is interesting to take a look at how leftists are attempting to destroy our military and one of the ways the left is trying to undermine our military is by attacking its recruiting base in high schools across the country. Activists are trying to persuade kids of military recruitment age to "opt out" from allowing their schools to provide the student's public information to military sources.

The anti-military left has also found a constant assistant in the MSM [Main Stream Media] toward this goal. Every few months the MSM comes out with articles highlighting military recruiting and invariably they also give free publicity to the anti-[m]ilitary groups trying to stop recruiting.

Warner Todd Huston, "MSM Killing Military Recruiting," *The Conservative Voice*, November 23, 2006. Reproduced by permission.

For example, a recent *USA Today* report, titled "Some opt out of military options," introduces us to a school in northern Illinois where a large number of parents, totaling about half the class, have signed forms to stop the school from sending the military their info—a trend that has grown there since at least 2004.

USA Today helpfully supplies a graphic showing the "Opt out" split in the school body. 2004 saw 2,126 opt outers in a student body of 4,505. 2,802 of 4,573 in 2005 and 2,920 out of 4,472 this school year. This stat shows a pretty steady growth toward the anti-military position.

It almost mirrors the voting trend north of Chicago in Lake County, Illinois, where the school is located.

Lincolnshire, Illinois, a northern suburb of the city of Chicago, is in Lake county. It broke close to even in the 2004 election with 50% going for Bush and 48% going for Kerry. And, while they voted overwhelmingly for Democrat Barack Obama in 2004, the rest of the votes were weighted Republican at least since the 2000 general election. But in this 2006 cycle, the GOP took a hit with Democratic votes gaining for most of the top offices, as it did in many areas of the country.

A Forum for the Left

But, what the *USA Today* article proves most clearly, is that the left is doing what it does best; organize. And they are organizing in an effort to undermine the U.S. military. The article covers several organizations that have organized to fight Military recruiters from having access to school records.

A quick perusal of some of the stories over the last couple of years—since the war in Iraq started—on military recruiting shows a constant drumbeat against the military.

Even cities have taken up the anti-military cause. The school board in San Francisco has recently banned the Junior

Reserve Officers' Training Corps from operating in city high schools, despite complaints from students, over the "don't ask, don't tell" that supposedly discriminates against gays. School board member, Eric Mar, was quoted as saying "... in many ways, we're preventing military values on students at the high-school level."

The reason I use this article as an example, though, is in the unusual aspect of it. It gives both sides of the argument where few others do. This article gives space to military spokesmen and gives some info to mitigate the attacks by the anti-military left. The most salient points being that the military isn't asking for any more information than colleges and Universities get from schools and that the military can get the student's info from other sources quite legally, anyway.

Still, we get a pretty detailed listing of several of the anti-military groups formed to mount an attack on the U.S. military's ability to recruit in schools. In that *USA Today* helps the anti-military as much as possible.

As I said, that mirrors the common drift of most of the stories on the issue of recruiting. A quick perusal of some of the stories over the last couple of years—since the war in Iraq started—on military recruiting shows a constant drumbeat against the military. Whether it be a dour report on the military missing its goals or the resistance being mounted in schools to disrupt military recruit efforts, these stories constantly show a heavy bias against the military.

A Few Examples

A writer from the Portland Oregonian gins up a tale about how military recruiter's misconduct "is a growing national problem as the military faces increasing pressure to hit recruiting targets during an unpopular war." (A story the subject of which that I proved to be pure hyperbole since the stats show an extremely low number of such cases. ....)

The San Francisco Chronicle delighted in reporting that the "U.S. is recruiting misfits for army—felons, racists, gang members fill in the ranks".

The stories show a mounting effort to undermine the U.S. military's recruitment efforts.

A 2005 story informs us that the army is having trouble because "Parents can opt to deny this information to recruiters, and antiwar groups are mounting a national effort to encourage them to do so."

Then there was the 2004 PBS story that highlighted the work of "the head of a local San Diego peace group which has serious problems with military recruitment at high schools."

In 2002, *Mother Jones Magazine* complained that military recruiters access to students "undercuts the authority of some local school districts, including San Francisco and Portland, Oregon, that have barred recruiters from schools on the grounds that the military discriminates against gays and lesbians."

In any case, the inference is clear. The stories show a mounting effort to undermine the U.S. military's recruitment efforts. Sadly, in this time of mounting security risks, one of the most threatening things that recruiters face seem not to be the prospect of new recruits being sent into combat, but teachers and unpatriotic parents telling their kids they don't have any duty to their country.

We have heard the sobriquet of "Greatest Generation" bestowed upon those who fought WWII [World War II]. One wonders what title these kinds of people might be saddled with in the decades to come? Perhaps the "Weakest Generation"? And, it would not be the mantle given to the youngsters who now serve, but their parent's generation, instead.

12

The Military Has Lowered Its Standards to Meet Recruiting Quotas

Fred Kaplan

Fred Kaplan is a regular contributing writer to Slate Magazine, *specifically writing the "War Stories" column for this publication. He is a former reporter and military correspondent for the* Boston Globe, *also serving as its Moscow bureau chief and New York bureau chief, and the author of* The Wizards of Armageddon. *He graduated from Oberlin College and has a PhD in political science from the Massachusetts Institute of Technology.*

Faced with falling short of its recruitment goals, the U.S. Army has been lowering its recruitment standards to improve its numbers. Not only has it been picking up more high school dropouts, it has also been enlisting more and more applicants who score in the lowest third of those taking the armed forces aptitude test. Unfortunately, in the military, intelligence does make a difference. Smarter soldiers means better performance and more lives saved in the field, as well as less monetary expense for the military.

Three months ago, I wrote that the war in Iraq was wrecking the U.S. Army, and since then the evidence has only mounted, steeply. Faced with repeated failures to meet its recruitment targets, the Army has had to lower its standards

Fred Kaplan, "GI Schmo: How Low Can Army Recruiters Go?" *Slate Magazine*, January 6, 2006, www.slate.com. Copyright © 2006 Washington post. Newsweek Interactive Co. LLC. Distributed by United Feature Syndicate, Inc. Reproduced by permission of the author.

dramatically. First it relaxed restrictions against high-school drop-outs. Then it started letting in more applicants who score in the lowest third on the armed forces aptitude test—a group, known as Category IV recruits, who have been kept to exceedingly small numbers, as a matter of firm policy, for the past 20 years. (There is also a Category V—those who score in the lowest 10^0 percentile. They have always been ineligible for service in the armed forces and, presumably, always will be.)

The bad news is twofold. First, the number of Category IV recruits is starting to skyrocket. Second, a new study compellingly demonstrates that, in all realms of military activity, intelligence does matter. Smarter soldiers and units perform their tasks better; dumber ones do theirs worse.

Until just last year, the Army had no trouble attracting recruits and therefore no need to dip into the dregs. As late as 2004, fully 92 percent of new Army recruits had graduated high school and just 0.6 percent scored Category IV on the military aptitude test.

Then came the spiraling casualties in Iraq, the diminishing popularity of the war itself, and the subsequent crisis in recruitment.

The Band-Aid Fix

In response to the tightening trends, on Sept. 20, 2005, the Defense Department released *DoD Instruction 1145.01*, which allows 4 percent of each year's recruits to be Category IV applicants—up from the 2 percent limit that had been in place since the mid-1980s. Even so, in October, the Army had such a hard time filling its slots that the floodgates had to be opened; *12 percent* of that month's active-duty recruits were Category IV. November was another disastrous month; Army officials won't even say how many Cat IV applicants they took in, except to acknowledge that the percentage was in "double digits."

(These officials insist that they will stay within the 4 percent limit *for the entire fiscal year*, which runs from October 2005 through September 2006. But given the extremely high percentage of Cat IVs recruited in the fiscal year's first two months, this pledge may be impossible to keep. . . .)

Some may wonder: So what? Can't someone who scores low on an aptitude test, even very low, go on to become a fine, competent soldier, especially after going through boot camp and training? No question. Some college drop-outs also end up doing very well in business and other professions. But in general, in the military no less than in the civilian world, the norm turns out to be otherwise.

In a *RAND Corp. report* commissioned by the office of the secretary of defense and published in 2005, military analyst Jennifer Kavanagh reviewed a spate of recent statistical studies on the various factors that determine military performance—experience, training, aptitude, and so forth—and concluded that aptitude is key. A force "made up of personnel with high AFQT [armed forces aptitude test] scores," Kavanagh writes, "contributes to a more effective and accurate team performance."

The evidence is overwhelming. Take tank gunners. You wouldn't think intelligence would have much effect on the ability to shoot straight, but apparently it does. Replacing a gunner who'd scored Category IV on the aptitude test (ranking in the 10–30 percentile) with one who'd scored Category IIIA (50–64 percentile) improved the chances of hitting targets by 34 percent. . . .

In another study cited by the RAND report, 84 three-man teams from the Army's active-duty signal battalions were given the task of making a communications system operational. Teams consisting of Category IIIA personnel had a 67 percent chance of succeeding. Those consisting of Category IIIB (who'd ranked in the 31–49 percentile on the aptitude test) had a 47 percent chance. Those with Category IV personnel had only a 29 percent chance.

The same study of signal battalions took soldiers who had just taken advanced individual training courses and asked them to troubleshoot a faulty piece of communications gear. They passed if they were able to identify at least two technical problems. Smarts trumped training. Among those who had scored Category I on the aptitude test (in the 93–99 percentile), 97 percent passed. Among those who'd scored Category II (in the 65–92 percentile), 78 percent passed. Category IIIA: 60 percent passed. Category IIIB: 43 percent passed. Category IV: a mere 25 percent passed.

Brains Needed Here

The pattern is clear: The higher the score on the aptitude test, the better the performance in the field. This is true for individual soldiers and for units. Moreover, the study showed that adding one high-scoring soldier to a three-man signals team boosted its chance of success by 8 percent (meaning that adding one low-scoring soldier boosts its chance of failure by a similar margin).

These are the soldiers that the Army has long shut out of its ranks; that it is now recruiting avidly, out of sheer desperation; and that—according to the military's own studies—seriously degrade the competence of every unit they end up joining.

Smarter also turns out to be cheaper. One study examined how many Patriot missiles various Army air-defense units had to fire in order to destroy 10 targets. Units with Category I personnel had to fire 20 missiles. Those with Category II had to fire 21 missiles. Category IIIA: 22. Category IIIB: 23. Category IV: 24 missiles. In other words, to perform the same task, Category IV units chewed up 20 percent more hardware than Category I units. For this particular task, since each *Patriot missile* costs about $2 million, they also chewed up $8 million more of the Army's procurement budget.

Some perspective here: Each year the Army recruits 80,000 new troops—which amount to 16 percent of its 500,000 active-duty soldiers. Even if 12 percent of recruits were Category IV, not just for October but for the entire coming year, they would swell the ranks of Cat IV soldiers *overall* by just 1.9 percent (0.12 x 0.16 = .0192).

Then again, viewed from another angle, this would double the Army's least desirable soldiers. These are the soldiers that the Army has long shut out of its ranks; that it is now recruiting avidly, out of sheer desperation; and that—according to the military's own studies—seriously degrade the competence of every unit they end up joining. No, things haven't gone to hell in a handbasket, but they're headed in that direction. Every Army officer knows this. And that's why many of them want the United States to get out of Iraq.

The Draft Is Needed to Maintain Military Superiority

Phillip Carter and Paul Glastris

Phillip Carter and Paul Glastris are both professionally associated with The Washington Monthly. *Carter is an attorney and former Army captain who writes about national security issues. Glastris is the publication's editor-in-chief.*

Iraq is unlike other countries to which the United States came, sponsored elections, and left behind a relatively stable and peaceful democracy (e.g., Germany, Japan, Bosnia, Kosovo). The present volunteer military force may not have the strength to secure peace in such a volatile environment. But that's not to say that America needs a bigger army. Rather, what it needs is a highly-trained active-duty force, backed up with a hefty-sized reserve of soldiers who can readily mobilize and provide massive surge capacity in the event of unpredictable war or unmanageable circumstance. At the end of the day, what America should rely on is a twenty-first-century-style draft of all eligible young persons.

The United States has occupied many foreign lands over the last half century—Germany and Japan in World War II, and, on a much smaller scale, Haiti, Bosnia, and Kosovo in the 1990s. In all these cases, we sponsored elections and handed-off to democratic governments control of countries that were relatively stable, secure, and reasonably peaceful.

Phillip Carter and Paul Glastris, "The Case for the Draft," *Washington Monthly*, vol. 37, March 2005. Copyright 2005 by Washington Monthly Publishing, LLC, 733 15th St. NW, Suite 520, Washington DC 20005. (202) 393-5155. Web site: www.washington monthly.com. Reproduced by permission.

In Iraq, we failed to do this, despite heroic efforts by U.S. and coalition troops. The newly-elected Iraqi government inherits a country in which assassinations, kidnappings, suicide bombings, pipeline sabotages, and beheadings of foreigners are daily occurrences. For the last eight months, the ranks of the insurgency have been growing faster than those of the security forces of the provisional Iraqi government—and an alarming number of those government forces are secretly working for the insurgency. American-led combat operations in Ramadi and Fallujah killed large numbers of the enemy, but at the price of fanning the flames of anti-American hatred and dispersing the insurrection throughout Iraq. Despite nearly two years of effort, American troops and civilian administrators have failed to restore basic services to much of the central part of the country where a majority of Iraqis live. The U.S. military has not even been able to secure the 7-mile stretch of highway leading from the Baghdad airport to the Green Zone where America's own embassy and the seat of the Iraqi government are headquartered.

Off to a Bad Start

How we got to this point is by now quite obvious. Even many of the war's strongest supporters admit that the Bush administration grievously miscalculated by invading Iraq with too few troops and then by stubbornly refusing to augment troop numbers as the country descended into violent mayhem after the fall of Saddam.

This analysis, of course, presumes that it was ever possible to invade and quickly pacify Iraq, given the country's religious-ethnic divisions and history of tyranny. But it also presumes that the fault is primarily one of judgment: that the president and key senior military officials made a mistake by accepting Defense Secretary Donald Rumsfeld's theory that a "transformed" American military can prevail in war without great masses of ground troops. That judgment was indeed foolish;

events have shown that, while a relatively modest American force can win a stunning battlefield victory, such a force is not enough to secure the peace.

America has a choice. It can be the world's superpower, or it can maintain the current all-volunteer military, but it probably can't do both.

But there's a deeper problem, one that any president who chose to invade a country the size of Iraq would have faced. In short, America's all-volunteer military simply cannot deploy and sustain enough troops to succeed in places like Iraq while still deterring threats elsewhere in the world. Simply adding more soldiers to the active duty force, as some in Washington are now suggesting, may sound like a good solution. But it's not, for sound operational and pragmatic reasons. America doesn't need a bigger standing army; it needs a deep bench of trained soldiers held in reserve who can be mobilized to handle the unpredictable but inevitable wars and humanitarian interventions of the future. And while there are several ways the all-volunteer force can create some extra surge capacity, all of them are limited.

The only effective solution to the manpower crunch is the one America has turned to again and again in its history: the draft. Not the mass combat mobilizations of World War II, nor the inequitable conscription of Vietnam—for just as threats change and war-fighting advances, so too must the draft. A modernized draft would demand that the privileged participate. It would give all who serve a choice over how they serve. And it would provide the military, on a "just in time" basis, large numbers of deployable ground troops, particularly the peacekeepers we'll need to meet the security challenges of the 21st century.

America has a choice. It can be the world's superpower, or it can maintain the current all-volunteer military, but it probably can't do both. . . .

Five Bad Options

In theory, there are several ways to get out of the military manpower bind we find ourselves in. In reality, there are inherent limits to almost all of them.

The first option—at least the one Democrats and moderate Republicans have talked most about—is to convince other countries to share the burden in Iraq. But that's not likely. Even if the security situation in Iraq improves and the Bush administration begins to share decision-making—something it's so far refused to do—European leaders would be extremely wary of trying to sell their citizens on sending troops to keep the peace in a war they expressly opposed. It may be possible to convince the Europeans and other developed nations to be more willing to contribute troops the next time there's an international need. But that, as we've seen, will require more U.S. troops, not fewer. Nor should it be the policy of the United States to have to rely on other countries' troops. We must be prepared to intervene unilaterally if necessary.

A second solution to the manpower crisis would be to rely more on private military contractors, whose use has exploded in recent years. Currently, more than 40,000 government contractors are on duty in Iraq, working in myriad jobs from security to reconstruction. The advantage of using contractors is that they provide surge capacity; they are hired only for the duration of an engagement. But according to Peter W. Singer, a research fellow at the Brookings Institution, these private armies also create problems. First, all costs considered, they're not necessarily less expensive for the military. Second, private military contractors often compete with the military for personnel, so any growth in these contractors usually results in tension between military retention and contractor recruiting efforts. Third, contractors operate in a legal gray area where their financial and accounting activities are heavily regulated, but their operations are barely looked at. It's one thing to contract for truck drivers; it's another to hire contractors to guard Afghan President Hamid Karzai or work as interrogation linguists in the Abu Ghraib prison because the military has too few commandos or linguists in its own ranks. The military has probably already pushed the contractor concept about as far as it will go; expecting much more surge capacity from private industry is probably unrealistic.

[T]he army is mainly comprised of healthy young people with high school degrees but no college plans. That pool is inherently limited, especially when the economy is heating up and there's a shooting war on.

Transforming Existing Forces

A third possibility might be to follow the advice of several cutting-edge military reformers to radically transform today's military. According to these reformers, today's force was drawn up for a bygone age of massed superpower armies; it does not reflect today's threats. These visionaries would downsize the Navy, scrap some of the Army's mechanized divisions, and in these and other ways free up tens of thousands of troops to be redeployed into "soldier centric" units capable of doing everything along the spectrum from humanitarian relief in Banda Aceh to combat patrols in Baghdad. Under pressure from the Iraq mission, the military has taken some steps in this direction—for instance, by retraining and reequipping some army artillery and air defense units into military police units. But such moves have been incremental in nature thus far; the true scope of the problem is orders of magnitude larger than the Pentagon's current solution. And some day, a war may come which requires all kinds of combat power—from large land-based formations to ships capable of sailing through the Taiwan strait to legions of peacekeepers. The military cannot build additional capability simply by playing a shell game with its personnel; at some point, it must genuinely add more soldiers too, and in large numbers.

A fourth option, and the most obvious one, would be to simply increase the size of the active-duty force. This too has been discussed. During the 2004 campaign, Sen. John Kerry called for increasing the active-duty force by 40,000 troops. More recently, a bipartisan group of hawkish defense intellectuals published an open letter on *The Weekly Standard* Web site calling on Congress to add 25,000 ground troops each year for the next several years. And the Pentagon has announced some money for extra troops in the administration's latest budget. The problem with such proposals is that they underestimate both current manpower needs and the cost of forcing the all-volunteer military to grow.

In theory, one can always lure the next recruit, or retain the next soldier, by offering a marginally higher monetary incentive—but in reality, there are practical limits to such measures. The pool of people who might be convinced to join the Army is mainly comprised of healthy young people with high school degrees but no college plans. That pool is inherently limited, especially when the economy is heating up and there's a shooting war on. Last year, despite signing bonuses in the tens of thousands and other perks, military recruiters had to lower entry standards to meet their enlistment goals. The active force met its recruiting targets for 2004, but the reserves have found themselves increasingly struggling to bring enough soldiers in the door.

But it's the long-term cost issues that most militate against making the all-volunteer force bigger. Generals today are fond of saying that you recruit a soldier, but you retain their families. One reason the Army has resisted Congress' attempts to raise its end strength is that it does not want to embrace all of the costs associated with permanently increasing the size of the military, because it sees each soldier as a 30-year commitment—both to the soldier and his (or her) family. According to the Congressional Budget Office, each soldier costs $99,000 per year—a figure which includes medical care, housing, and family benefits.

When Size Matters

The United States does not necessarily need a massive standing military all the time. What it needs is a highly trained professional force of a certain size—what we have right now is fine—backed by a massive surge capacity of troops in reserve to quickly augment the active-duty force in times of emergency. Sure, right now, the Army is light several hundred thousand deployable ground troops. But over the long term, the demands of Iraq will subside, the need for troops will decline, and it could be another decade or two before another mission that big comes along.

The problem is that under the all-volunteer system it's hard to fix the short-term problem (too few troops now) without creating long-term problems (too many troops later). And so, paying for the salaries and benefits and families of 50,000 or 500,000 extra soldiers on active duty over the course of their careers doesn't, from a military standpoint, make sense. Politically, it would put the senior military leadership in the position of convincing the American people to keep military budgets extremely high to pay for a huge standing army that isn't being used and might not be for years. It might be possible now to convince the public to add another 100,000 soldiers (annual cost: about $10 billion in personnel costs alone, not including equipment and training). But the generals rightly worry that this support will evaporate after Iraq stabilizes. Indeed, Americans have a long tradition dating back to the writing of [the] Constitution, of refusing to support a large standing military unless the need is apparent. (The public paid for a much bigger all-volunteer military in the 1970s and 1980s, but only because of the obvious need to deter a massive Soviet army from threatening Europe; after the Berlin Wall fell, both political parties supported big cuts in troop strength). What we really need is the capability to rapidly mobilize and deploy a half million troops to project U.S. power abroad, and to be able to sustain them indefinitely while maintaining a reserve with which to simultaneously engage other enemies.

A fifth option would be to build this surge capacity into the reserves, instead of the active force. Under this plan, which some military personnel planners are already discussing, the army would radically bump up enlistment bonuses and other incentives to lure vastly more young people directly into the reserves than are being recruited now. Such a plan would have the advantage of creating the surge capacity the nation needs without saddling the nation with a large, standing professional army. But the disadvantages are substantial, too. For such a plan to work, the military would have to make a commitment, which thus far it never has, to fix the legendary resources problems and anemic readiness of the reserves. A great many reservists have gone through the crucible of combat in Afghanistan and Iraq, and yet still cope with vehicles that lack armor, weapons older than they are, and a paucity of training dollars. Also, the army would always (and rightly) insist that signing bonuses for reservists be substantially below those offered to active-duty recruits. And even if bonuses and other renumeration for both the active-duty and the reserves were to rise substantially, it is hard to see how the reserves could lure in a sufficient number of recruits without significantly lowering admissions standards. The real advantage of the all-volunteer force is its quality. If the military tries to recruit so many soldiers that it must substantially lower its entry requirements, then the all-volunteer force will lose its qualitative edge. This decrease in quality will have a cascade effect on discipline within the ranks, degrading combat effectiveness for these units.

A Modern Proposal

That leaves one option left for providing the military with sufficient numbers of high-quality deployable ground forces: conscription. America has nearly always chosen this option to staff its military in times of war. Today, no leading politician in either party will come anywhere near the idea—the draft having replaced Social Security as the third rail of American politics. This will have to change if the United States is to remain the world's preeminent power.

> *[A]ny American, liberal or conservative, ought to have moral qualms about basing our nation's security on an all-volunteer force drawn disproportionately, as ours is, from America's lower socioeconomic classes.*

Traditional conscription has its obvious downsides. On a practical level, draftees tend to be less motivated than volunteers. Because they serve for relatively short periods of time (typically two years), any investment made in their training is lost to the military once the draftees return to civilian life. And despite the current manpower shortage, there's no foreseeable scenario in which all 28 million young Americans currently of draft age would be needed.

Above all else, there's the serious ethical problem that conscription means government compelling young adults to risk death, and to kill—an act of the state that seems contrary to the basic notions of liberty which animate our society.

In practice, however, our republic has decided many times throughout its history that a draft was necessary to protect those basic liberties. Even if you disagreed with the decision to invasion of Iraq, or think the president's rhetoric is demagogic and his policies disastrous, it is hard to argue that Islamic terrorism isn't a threat to freedom and security, at home and abroad. Moreover, any American, liberal or conservative, ought to have moral qualms about basing our nation's security on an all-volunteer force drawn disproportionately, as ours is, from America's lower socioeconomic classes. And the cost of today's war is being borne by an extremely narrow slice of America. Camp Pendleton, Calif., home to the 1st Marine Expeditionary Force, is also home to approximately one-seventh of the U.S. fatalities from Iraq. In theory, our democracy will not fight unpopular wars because the people who must bear the casualties can impose their will on our elected leaders to end a war they do not support. But when such a small fraction of America shoulders the burden—and pays the cost—of America's wars, this democratic system breaks down.

Nor are the practical considerations of a draft impossible to overcome. A draft lottery, of the kind that existed in the peacetime draft of the 1950s, with no exemptions for college students, would provide the military an appropriate and manageable amount of manpower without the class inequities that poisoned the national culture during Vietnam. Such a system, however, would not avoid the problem of flooding the military with less-than-fully-motivated conscripts.

How a Modern Draft Should Function

A better solution would fix the weaknesses of the all-volunteer force without undermining its strengths. Here's how such a plan might work. Instead of a lottery, the federal government would impose a requirement that no four-year college or university be allowed to accept a student, male or female, unless and until that student had completed a 12-month to two-year term of service. Unlike an old-fashioned draft, this 21st-century service requirement would provide a vital element of personal choice. Students could choose to fulfill their obligations in any of three ways: in national service programs like AmeriCorps (tutoring disadvantaged children), in homeland security assignments (guarding ports), or in the military. Those who chose the latter could serve as military police officers, truck drivers, or other non-combat specialists requiring only modest levels of training. (It should be noted that the Army currently offers two-year enlistments for all of these jobs, as well as for the infantry.) They would be deployed as needed for peacekeeping or nation-building missions. They would serve for 12-months to two years, with modest follow-on reserve obligations.

Whichever option they choose, all who serve would receive modest stipends and GI Bill-type college grants. Those who sign up for lengthier and riskier duty, however, would receive higher pay and larger college grants. Most would no doubt pick the less dangerous options. But some would certainly select the military—out of patriotism, a sense of adventure, or to test their mettle. Even if only 10 percent of the one-million young people who annually start at four-year colleges and universities were to choose the military option, the armed forces would receive 100,000 fresh recruits every year. These would be motivated recruits, having chosen the military over other, less demanding forms of service. And because they would all be college-grade and college-bound, they would have—to a greater extent than your average volunteer recruit—the savvy and inclination to pick up foreign languages and other skills that are often the key to effective peacekeeping work.

A 21st-century draft like this would create a cascading series of benefits for society. It would instill a new ethic of service in that sector of society, the college-bound, most likely to reap the fruits of American prosperity. It would mobilize an army of young people for vital domestic missions, such as helping a growing population of seniors who want to avoid nursing homes but need help with simple daily tasks like grocery shopping. It would give more of America's elite an experience of the military. Above all, it would provide the all-important surge capacity now missing from our force structure, insuring that the military would never again lack for manpower. And it would do all this without requiring any American to carry a gun who did not choose to do so.

The war in Iraq has shown us, and the world, many things: the bloody costs of inept leadership; the courage of the average American soldier; the hunger for democracy among some of the earth's most oppressed people. But perhaps more than anything, Iraq has shown that our military power has limits. As currently constituted, the U.S. military can win the wars, but it cannot win the peace, nor can it commit for the long term to the stability and security of a nation such as Iraq. Our enemies have learned this, and they will use that knowledge to their advantage in the next war to tie us down and bleed us until we lose the political will to fight.

If America wishes to retain its mantle of global leadership, it must develop a military force structure capable of persevering under these circumstances. Fortunately, we know how to build such a force. We have done it many times in the past. The question is: Do we have the will to do so again?

14

Only Unjust Wars
Require a Draft

Ron Paul

Ron Paul serves as Representative of the Fourteenth District of Texas in the U.S. House of Representatives, and is a 2008 presidential candidate seeking nomination by the Republican Party. During the Vietnam War, he was a flight surgeon in the U.S. Air Force. In Congress, he has served as member of the Committee on International Relations, among others.

War itself is a doubtful necessity at best; a costly waste of life and liberty at worst. U.S. presidents have established a long history of deceiving the public to justify war or garner support for ill-conceived military conflict. This is certainly true of the Iraq war, despite its staggering cost in human casualties and dollars. Few persons readily volunteer for service in an unjust, unnecessary war such as this, therefore the possibility of a military draft looms on the horizon. But conscription is always unfair and discriminatory: it takes our youthful best to fight the wars conceived by politicians who seek the glory of victory without personally paying any price. Conscription is an instrument of tyranny that men of principle should oppose.

The ultimate cost of war is almost always the loss of liberty. True defensive wars and revolutionary wars against tyrants may preserve or establish a free society, as did our war against the British. But these wars are rare. Most wars are unnecessary, dangerous, and cause senseless suffering with little

Ron Paul, "Pro & Con: Congress Reinstating the Military Draft?" *Congressional Digest*, May 2004, pp. 143–147. Reproduced by permission.

being gained. Loss of liberty and life on both sides has been the result of most of the conflicts throughout the ages. The current war in which we find ourselves clearly qualifies as one of those unnecessary and dangerous wars. To get the people to support ill-conceived wars the Nation's leaders employ grand schemes of deception.

A History of Deception

Woodrow Wilson orchestrated our entry into World War I by first promising in the election of 1916 to keep us out of the European conflict, then a few months later pressured and maneuvered the Congress into declaring war against Germany. Whether it was the Spanish-American War before that or all the wars since, U.S. Presidents have deceived the people to gain popular support for ill-conceived military ventures.

Wilson wanted the war and immediately demanded conscription to fight it. He didn't have the guts to even name the program a military draft, and instead in a speech before Congress calling for war advised the army should be "chosen upon the principle of universal liability, to service." Most Americans at the time of the declaration didn't believe actual combat troops would be sent. What a dramatic change from this early perception when the people endorsed the war to the carnage that followed and the later disillusionment with Wilson and his grand scheme for world government under the League of Nations, The American people rejected this gross new entanglement, reflecting a somewhat healthier age than the one in which we find ourselves today.

But when it comes to war, the principle of deception lives on and the plan for "universal liability to serve" once again is raising its ugly head. The dollar cost of the current war is already staggering, yet plans are being made to drastically expand the human cost by forcing conscription on the young men (and maybe women) who have no ax to grind with the Iraqi people and want no part of this fight. Hundreds of

Americans have already been killed and thousands more wounded and crippled while thousands of others will suffer from new and deadly war-related illnesses not yet identified.

We were told we had to support this preemptive war against Iraq because Saddam Hussein had weapons of mass destruction and to confront the al Qaeda. It was said our national security depended on it. But all these dangers were found not to exist in Iraq. It was implied that those who did not support this Iraqi invasion were un-American and unpatriotic.

Since the original reasons for the war never existed, it is now claimed that we're there to make Iraq a Western-style democracy and to spread Western values. And besides, it's argued, it's nice that Saddam Hussein has been removed from power. But does the mere existence of evil somewhere in the world justify preemptive war at the expense of the American people?

Setting the Stage For A Draft

These after-the-fact excuses for invasion and occupation of a sovereign nation direct attention away from the charge that this war was encouraged by the military industrial complex, war profiteering, control of natural resources (oil), and a neocon agenda of American hegemony with a desire to redraw the borders of the countries of the Middle East.

The inevitable failure of such a seriously flawed foreign policy cannot be contemplated by those who have put so much energy into this occupation. The current quagmire prompts calls from many for escalation with more troops being sent to Iraq. Many of our Reservists and National Guardsmen cannot wait to get out and have no plans to re-enlist.

To get more troops, the draft will likely be reinstituted. The implicit prohibition of "involuntary servitude" by the Thirteenth Amendment to the Constitution has already been ignored many times, so few will challenge the constitutionality of the coming draft. Unpopular wars invite conscription. Volunteers disappear, as well they should. A truly defensive, just war prompts popular support.

A conscripted, unhappy soldier is better off in the long run than the slaves of old since the "enslavement" is only temporary. But in the short run, the draft may well turn out to be more deadly and degrading as one is forced to commit life and limb to a less than worthy cause—like teaching democracy to unwilling and angry Arabs. Slaves were safer in that their owners had an economic interest in protecting their lives. Life endangerment for a soldier is acceptable policy and that's why they are needed. Too often though, our men and women who are exposed to the hostilities of war and welcomed initially are easily forgotten after the fighting ends.

There Is No Justification For A Draft

It is said we go about the world waging war to promote peace, and yet the price paid is rarely weighed against the failed efforts to make the world a better place. But justifying conscription to promote the cause of liberty is one of the most bizarre notions ever conceived by man.

Forced servitude with risk of death and serious injury as a price to live free makes no sense. By what right does anyone have to sacrifice the lives of others for some cause of questionable value?

Without conscription, unpopular wars are much more difficult to fight.

It's said that the 18-year-old owes it to his country. Hogwash. It could just as easily be argued that a 50-year-old chicken-hawk who promotes war and places the danger on the innocent young owes a heck of a lot more to the country than the 18-year-old being denied his liberty for a cause that has no justification.

All drafts are unfair. All 18- and 19-year-olds are never needed. By its very nature, a draft must be discriminatory. All drafts hit the most vulnerable as the elitists learn quickly how to avoid the risks of combat.

The dollar cost of war and the economic hardship is great in all wars and cannot be minimized. War is never economically beneficial except for those in position to profit from war expenditures.

But the great tragedy of war is the careless disregard for civil liberties of our own people. Abuse of German and Japanese Americans in World War I and World War II is well known. But the real sacrifice comes with conscription—forcing a small number of young vulnerable citizens to fight the wars that old men and women, who seek glory in military victory without themselves being exposed to danger, promote. These are wars with neither purpose nor moral justification and too often are not even declared by the Congress.

Choose Liberty, Not Tyranny

Without conscription, unpopular wars are much more difficult to fight. Once the draft was undermined in the 1960s and early 1970s, the Vietnam war came to an end.

But most importantly, liberty cannot be preserved by tyranny. A free society must always resort to volunteers. Tyrants think nothing of forcing men to fight and die in wrongheaded wars; a true fight for survival and defense of one's homeland I'm sure would elicit the assistance of every able-bodied man and woman. This is not the case for wars of mischief far away from home in which we so often have found ourselves in the past century.

One of the worst votes that an elected official could ever cast would be to institute a military draft to fight an illegal war, if that individual himself maneuvered to avoid military service. But avoiding the draft on principle qualifies oneself to work hard to avoid all unnecessary war and oppose the draft for all others.

A government that's willing to enslave a portion of its people to fight an unjust war can never be trusted to protect the liberties of its own citizens. The end can never justify the means, no matter what the neo-cons say.

15

All Americans Should Be Recruited to Serve Society

William A. Galston

William A. Galston is Interim Dean of the University of Maryland's School of Public Policy. He previously served as Deputy Assistant to President Bill Clinton for Domestic Policy. Galston has written several books, including The Practice of Liberal Pluralism.

During the Vietnam War (1959–1975) the draft was widely considered unfair, and this is largely to blame for the present anti-draft sentiment. Despite a good job done by our volunteer forces, the military has created a spectator audience of non-volunteers. This, in turn, creates the much larger question of what each person should do to become a good citizen. The all-volunteer force should include other contributions from non-military citizens. A true democracy involves the equal sharing of burdens in return for an overwhelmingly worthy benefit.

In the wake of September 11, [2001] the United States has undertaken a range of new and expanded military commitments, especially in Central Asia and the Middle East. The military occupation of Iraq is likely to last longer, and require larger forces, than civilian leaders in the Department of Defense had predicted prior to the war. The rising demands on U.S. military personnel, including lengthy overseas deployments and the increased risk of casualties, may well put pres-

William A. Galston, "Thinking About the Draft," *Public Interest*, Winter 2004. Copyright © 2004 by National Affairs, Inc. Reproduced by permission of the author.

sure on current recruitment strategies. This is an appropriate moment, then, to review the military manpower decisions we made a generation ago.

The Vietnam-era military draft was widely regarded as arbitrary and unfair, and it was held responsible for dissension within the military as well as the wider society. In the aftermath of the military failure in Vietnam, the United States made a historic decision to end the draft and institute the All-Volunteer Force (AVF). On one level, it's hard to argue with success. The formula of high-quality volunteers and intensive training plus investment in state-of-the-art equipment has produced by far the most formidable military in history. Evidence suggests that the military's performance, especially since 1990, has bolstered public trust and confidence. For example, a recent Gallup survey of public-opinion trends since the end of the Vietnam War in 1975 indicates that whereas the percentage of Americans expressing confidence in religious leaders fell from 68 to 45, and from 40 to 29 for members of Congress, those expressing confidence in the military rose from under 30 to 78 percent. Among 18-to-29 year-olds, the confidence level rose from 20 percent to 64 percent. These figures reflect public sentiment in late 2002, before the U.S. military victory in Iraq.

Less Palpable Costs

These gains in institutional performance and public confidence are impressive and significant, but they hardly end the discussion. The organization of the military is closely related to larger issues of citizenship and civic life. And here the decision in favor of the AVF has entailed significant costs. First, the AVF reflects, and has contributed to the development of, what I call "optional citizenship," the belief that being a citizen involves rights without responsibilities and that we need do for our country only what we choose to do. Numerous studies have documented the rise of a highly individualistic culture in contemporary America. Many young people today believe that being a good person—decent, kind, caring, and tolerant—is all it takes to be a good citizen. This duty-free understanding of citizenship is comfortable and undemanding; it is also profoundly mistaken.

Second, the AVF contributes to a kind of "spectatorial citizenship"—the premise that good citizens need not be active and can simply allow others to do the public's work on their behalf. This spectatorial outlook makes it possible to decouple the question of whether we as a nation should choose to engage militarily from the question of whether I would participate in such an endeavor.

In a discussion with his students during the Gulf War, Cheyney Ryan, professor of philosophy at the University of Oregon, was struck by "how many of them saw no connection between whether the country should go to war and whether they would . . . be willing to fight in it." A similar disconnection exists today. Young adults have been more supportive of the war in Iraq than any other age group (with more than 70 percent in favor), but recent surveys have found an equal percentage would refuse to participate themselves.

Finally, the AVF has contributed to a widening gap between the orientation and experience of military personnel and that of the citizenry as a whole. This remains a contested issue, but some facts are not in dispute. First, since the inauguration of the AVF, the share of officers identifying themselves as Republican has nearly doubled, from 33 percent to 64 percent. (To be sure, officers were always technically volunteers, but the threat of the draft significantly affected the willingness of young men to volunteer for officer candidacy.) Second, and more significantly, the share of elected officials with military experience has declined sharply. From 1900 through 1975, the percentage of members of Congress who were veterans was always higher than that of their peers in the population at large. Since the mid 1990s, the congressional percentage has been lower than that of the general public, and it continues to fall.

Lack of military experience does not necessarily imply hostility to the military. But it does reflect ignorance of the nature of military service, as well as diminished capacity and confidence to assess critically the claims that military leaders make. It is no accident that of all the post-war presidents, [former general] Dwight Eisenhower was the most capable of saying no to the military's strategic assessments and requests for additional resources.

Responsible Citizenship

For these reasons, among others, I believe that we should review and revise the decision made 30 years ago to institute an all-volunteer armed force. I hasten to add that I do not favor re-instituting anything like the Vietnam-era draft. It is hard to see how a reasonable person could prefer that fatally flawed system to today's arrangements. The question, rather, is whether feasible reforms could preserve the gains of the past 30 years while more effectively promoting an active, responsible citizenship among all Americans.

Everyone who receives the protection of society owes a return for the benefit, and the fact of living in society renders it indispensable that each should be bound to observe a certain line of conduct toward the rest.

My suggestion, however, faces a threshold objection, one that is widely shared by conservatives and liberals alike. Any significant shift back toward a mandatory system of military manpower, it is said, would represent an abuse of state power. In a recent article appearing in the New Republic, Judge Richard Posner enlists John Stuart Mill as an ally in the cause of classical liberalism—a theory of limited government that provides an "unobtrusive framework for private activities." Limited government so conceived, Posner asserts, "has no ideology, no 'projects,' but is really just an association for mutual protection." Posner celebrates the recent emergence of what he calls the "Millian center"—a form of politics that (unlike the socialist Left) embraces economic liberty and (unlike cultural conservatives on the Right) endorses personal liberty, and he deplores modern communitarianism's critique of untrammeled personal liberty in the name of the common good. High on Posner's bill of particulars against many communitarians is their recommendation to reinstitute a draft.

Before engaging Posner's argument, I should note that his attempt to appropriate Mill's *On Liberty* to oppose conscription is deeply misguided. This is clear if one looks at a few of the opening sentences from the fourth chapter, "Of the Limits to the Authority of Society Over the Individual":

> Everyone who receives the protection of society owes a return for the benefit, and the fact of living in society renders it indispensable that each should be bound to observe a certain line of conduct toward the rest. This conduct consists, first, in not injuring the interests of one another, or rather certain interests which, either by express legal provision or by tacit understanding, ought to be considered as rights; and secondly, in each person's bearing his share (to be fixed on some equitable principle) of the labors and sacrifices incurred for defending the society or its members from injury and molestation. These conditions society is justified in enforcing at all costs to those who endeavor to withhold fulfillment.

Clearly, Mill's liberalism has little to do with Posner's "Millian center." Be that as it may, let's take a closer look at Posner's argument. Posner contends that "conscription could be described as a form of slavery, in the sense that a conscript is a person deprived of the ownership of his own labor." If slavery is immoral, runs the argument, so is the draft. In a similar vein, the philosopher Robert Nozick once contended that "taxation of earnings from labor is on a par with forced labor." (If Nozick were right, then the AVF that Posner supports, funded as it is with tax dollars, could also be described as on a par with forced labor.)

Both Posner's and Nozick's arguments prove too much. If each individual's ownership of his or her own labor is seen as absolute, then society as such becomes impossible, because no political community can operate without resources, which must ultimately come from someone. History has proven that no polity of any size can subsist through voluntary contributions alone; the inevitable free-riders must be compelled by law to do their share.

One might object, reasonably enough, that this argument illustrates the difference between taxation and conscription: While a political community is inconceivable without taxation, it is demonstrably sustainable without conscription. It is one thing to restrict self-ownership of labor out of necessity, but a very different matter to restrict it out of choice. The problem is that this argument proves too little. Posner concedes that "there are circumstances in which military service is an obligation of citizenship." But there are no circumstances in which slavery is an obligation of citizenship. Moreover, it is not morally impermissible to volunteer for military service. But it is rightly forbidden to voluntarily place oneself in slavery. Therefore, slavery and military service must differ in kind, not degree. Furthermore, if there are circumstances in which military service is an obligation of citizenship, then the state is justified in enforcing that obligation through conscription. Notwithstanding the libertarian instincts of many Americans, a legitimate government cannot be said to have exceeded its rightful authority by implementing a mandatory system of military recruitment.

Theory vs. Reality

But this is not the end of the argument, for Posner has a broader agenda. He rejects the claim, advanced by Harvard political theorist Michael Sandel and other communitarians, that substituting market for nonmarket services represents a degrading "commodification" of social and civic life. Indeed, Posner celebrates what communitarians deplore. "Commodification promotes prosperity," he informs us, "and prosperity alleviates social ills." Posner also claims that communitarian theory is incapable of drawing a line between matters that rightly belong within the scope of the market and those that do not. Posner's defense of the cash nexus is exposed to precisely the same objection. Let me offer a series of examples designed to help delimit the proper sphere of nonmarket relations, of which military service is one.

Paying people to obey the law: Suppose we offered individuals a "compliance bonus"—a cash payment awarded at the end of each year they were not convicted of a felony or significant misdemeanor. It's not hard to imagine situations in which the benefits of this policy (measured in reduced enforcement costs) would outweigh the outlays for bonuses. What, if anything, is wrong with this? At least two things: First, it alters for the worse the expressive meaning of law. In a legitimate order, criminal law represents an authoritative declaration of the behavior the members of society expect of one another. The authoritativeness of the law is supposed to be a sufficient condition for obeying it, and internalizing the sense of law as authoritative is supposed to be a sufficient motive for obedience. To offer compliance payments is to contradict the moral and motivational sufficiency of the law.

Second, payment for compliance constitutes a moral version of Gresham's law: Lower motives will tend to drive out higher motives, and the more comfortable motives will tend to drive out the more demanding ones. When those who are inclined to obey the law for its own sake see others receiving compensation, they are likely to question the reasonableness of their conduct and to begin demanding payment themselves.

While compensating individuals for mandatory military service is in itself unobjectionable, the AVF sends a misleading message. It suggests that the military is a career like any other, to be chosen on the basis of inclination and reward. Compensation as the key incentive or motive implies, wrongly, that military service is something to be bought and sold in the market, not part of the fundamental social contract.

Paying citizens for jury duty: Consider the analogy (or disanalogy) between national defense and domestic law enforcement. The latter is divided into two subcategories: voluntary service (there is no draft for police officers) and mandatory service (e.g., jury duty). Our current system of military manpower is all "police" and no "jury." If we conducted domestic law enforcement on our current military model, we'd have what might be called the "All-Volunteer Jury," in which we'd essentially buy the number of jurors necessary for the law enforcement system to function.

[I]t is important for all citizens to understand that citizenship is an office, not simply a status. As an office, citizenship entails both rights and duties.

There are two compelling reasons why our jury system is not run on a volunteer basis. First, citizens who self-select for jury duty would be unlikely to be representative of the population as a whole. Individuals who incur high opportunity costs (those who are gainfully employed, for example) would choose not to serve. The same considerations that militate against forced exclusion of racial and ethnic groups from jury pools would weigh equally against voluntary self-exclusion based upon income or employment status. We should ask ourselves why these considerations do not apply to the composition of the military.

Second, it is important for all citizens to understand that citizenship is an office, not simply a status. As an office, citizenship entails both rights and duties. Service on juries is itself simultaneously a right, in the sense that there is a strong presumption against exclusion, and a duty, in the sense that there is a strong presumption against evasion. The same could be said of military service.

Paying foreigners to do our fighting for us: It could be argued that we would do as well or better to hire foreigners (call it the "All-Mercenary Armed Forces") as kings and princes did regularly during the eighteenth century. The cost might well be lower, and the military performance just as high. Besides, if we hire foreigners to pick our grapes, why shouldn't we hire them to do our fighting? There is, of course, a practical problem, discussed by Machiavelli among others: a pure cash nexus would likely encourage opportunistic side-switching when individuals are presented with a better offer. In addition, what Abraham Lincoln called the "last full measure of devotion" would be less likely to be forthcoming from mercenaries.

Beyond these practical considerations lies a moral intuition: Even if a mercenary army were reliable and effective, it would be wrong, even shameful, to use our wealth to bribe noncitizens to do our fighting for us. This is something we ought to do for ourselves, as a self-respecting people. A similar moral principle should apply in the purely domestic sphere, among citizens.

Paying other citizens to do our fighting for us: Consider military recruitment during the Civil War. In April 1861, President Lincoln called for, and quickly received, 75,000 volunteers. But the expectation of a quick and easy Union victory was soon dashed, and the first conscription act was passed in March 1863. The act contained two opt-out provisions: An individual facing conscription could pay a fee of $300 to avoid a specific draft notice; and an individual could avoid service for the entire war by paying a substitute to volunteer for three years.

This law created a complex pattern of individual incentives and unanticipated social outcomes, including anticonscription riots among urban workers. Setting these aside, was there anything wrong in principle with these opt-out provisions? One argument against such provisions was their obvious distributional unfairness: The well-off could afford to avoid military service, while the poor and working classes could not. Historian James McPherson observes that the slogan "a rich man's fight, but a poor man's war" had a powerful impact, particularly among impoverished Irish laborers already chafing against the contempt with which they were regarded by the Protestant elite. Second, even if income and wealth had been more nearly equal, there was something unprincipled in the idea that dollars could purchase exemption from an important civic duty. As McPherson notes, this provision enjoyed a poor reputation after the Civil War, and the designers of the World War I-era Selective Service Act were careful not to repeat it.

Widening the Gap

What is the difference between the use of personal monetary resources to opt out of military service and the impact of such resources on the decision to opt in? In both practical and moral terms the difference is less than the defenders of the current system would have us believe. To begin with, the move to the AVF has had a profound effect on the educational and class composition of the U.S. military. During World War II and the Korean War—indeed, through the early 1960s—roughly equal percentages of high school and college graduates served in the military, and about one-third of college graduates were in the enlisted (that is, non-officer) ranks. Today, enlisted men and women are rarely college graduates, and elite colleges other than the service academies are far less likely to produce military personnel of any rank, officer or enlisted. As a lengthy *New York Times* feature story recently put it, today's military "mirrors a working-class America." Of the first 28 soldiers to die in Iraq, only one came from a family that could be described as well-off.

Many have argued that this income disparity is a positive reflection of a military that extends good career opportunities to young men and women whose prospects are otherwise limited. There is some merit to this argument, of course. But the current system purchases economic mobility at the expense of social integration. Today's privileged young people tend to grow up hermetically sealed off from the rest of society. Episodic volunteering in soup kitchens doesn't really break the seal. Military service is one of the few experiences that can.

The separation is more than economic. The sons and daughters of the middle and upper classes grow up in a cultural milieu in which certain assumptions tend to be taken for granted. Often, college experiences reinforce these views rather than challenging them. Since the Vietnam War, moreover, many elite colleges and universities have held the military at arm's length, ending ROTC curricula and banning campus-based military recruitment. As a Vietnam-era draftee, I can attest to the role military service plays in expanding mutual awareness across cultural lines. This process is not always pleasant or pretty, but it does help to bridge the gap between the privileged and lower classes.

In an evocative letter to his sons, Brookings scholar Stephen Hess reflects on his experiences as a draftee and defends military service as a vital socializing experience for children from fortunate families. His argument is instructive:

> Being forced to be the lowest rank ... serving for long enough that you can't clearly see "the light at the end of the tunnel," is as close as you will ever come to being a member

of society's underclass. To put it bluntly, you will feel in your gut what it means to be at the bottom of the heap.

It is a matter not just of compassion, but of respect:

The middle class draftee learns to appreciate a lot of talents (and the people who have them) that are not part of the lives you have known, and, after military duty, will know again for the rest of your lives. This will come from being thrown together with—and having to depend on—people who are very different from you and your friends.

A modern democracy, in short, combines legal equality with economic and social stratification. It is far from inevitable, or even natural, that democratic leaders who are drawn disproportionately from the upper ranks of society will adequately understand the experiences or respect the contributions of those from the lower. Integrative experiences are needed to bring this about. In a society in which economic class largely determines residence and education and in which the fortunate will not willingly associate with the rest, only nonvoluntary institutions cutting across class lines can hope to provide such experiences.

Uncle Sam Wants You

The inference I draw from the foregoing analysis is this: To the extent that circumstances permit, we should move toward a system of universal 18-month service for all high school graduates (and in the case of dropouts, all 18 year-olds) who are capable of performing it. Within the limits of the ceiling on military manpower, those subject to this new system would be assigned to either military or full-time civilian service. (If all military slots were filled, then some form of civilian service would be the only option.) The cost of enacting this proposal (a minimum of $60 billion per year) would certainly slow the pace of implementation and might well set limits on its final scope. The best response to these constraints would be a lottery from which none except those unfit to serve would be exempt.

It might be argued that a program of this sort would have little if any effect on the armed forces, which would continue to draw their manpower from the current stream of volunteers. That may be the case if the military doesn't expand during the next decade. But there are reasons to believe that it will. It is quickly becoming evident that the post-war occupation of Iraq will require more troops and last longer than administration officials had predicted. As an interim response, the military has already moved away from the all-volunteer principle. The U.S. Marine Corps has frozen enlistments for all of the 175,000 personnel currently on active duty. Marines whose period of voluntary enlistment has expired are required to remain in the service, on active duty, until the freeze expires. Other services have imposed similar if more limited freezes. It is possible, moreover, that the prospect of being sent to Iraq as part of a vulnerable long-term occupation force will depress the number of voluntary enlistments, especially in the Army and Marines.

A less purely voluntary system of military and civilian service might well garner popular support. For example, a 2002 survey sponsored by the Center for Information and Research on Civic Learning and Engagement (CIRCLE) found that over 60 percent of Americans across lines of sex, race, ethnicity, partisan affiliation, and ideology would support a plan that allows draftees to choose between civilian and military service. Still, it is plausible that intense opposition on the part of young adults and their parents could stymie such a change. Assuming that this is the case, there are some feasible interim steps that could yield civic rewards.

Former Secretary of the Navy John Lehman has suggested eliminating the current bias of military recruiters who favor career personnel over those willing to serve for shorter periods. As Lehman puts it, we should "actively seek to attract the most talented from all backgrounds with service options that allow them to serve their country . . . without having to commit to six to ten years' active duty." He makes a strong case that this change would markedly increase the number of young men and women from elite colleges and universities who would be willing to undertake military service. Coupled with a more accommodating stance toward the military on the part of academic administrators, this new recruitment strategy could make a real difference.

In a similar vein, the Progressive Policy Institute's Marc Magee has recently proposed reorganizing the current Selective Service registration system into a National Service System that would encourage young Americans to serve their country. Under this proposal, which would include both men and women, individuals who commit to serve in a military or civilian capacity would be exempt from any future draft. To make service more meaningful and attractive, the short-term military enlistment program would be expanded, an enlarged AmeriCorps would be linked more closely to homeland security, and a substantial portion of a scaled-up Peace Corps would be reoriented towards changing the conditions overseas that breed terror.

It would be wrong to oversell the civic benefits that might accrue from the revisions to the AVF that I propose, let alone the more modest steps I have just sketched. Still, enhanced contact between the sorts of young people who provide the bulk of today's volunteers and the sons and daughters of the privileged upper and middle classes would represent real progress. The sacrifices demanded of those who perform military service should be borne more equitably than they currently are. This is especially the case today as the military responsibilities of the United States appear to be on the rise. If reconsidering a decision about military manpower made three decades ago could yield even a fraction of these civic dividends while preserving the military effectiveness of the current system, it would be well worth the effort.

16

Do Not Bring Back the Draft

Rick Jahnkow

Rick Jahnkow is a contributing writer for various liberal Web sites and works for two San Diego-based anti-militarist organizations: the Project on Youth and Non-Military Opportunities, and the Committee Opposed to Militarism and the Draft.

Some among liberals and progressives, long a source of opposition to the draft in particular, have begun agitating to bring back the draft. They argue that a new draft could be more fair than drafts of the past, and that by drafting Americans from all walks of life, the military would be transformed into a more representative organization that would also be more difficult to politically justify sending into battle. These are false beliefs. History has shown that drafts create large standing armies that make it easier to wage war, not harder. Rather than transforming the character of the military, drafts spread military culture into society at large. Furthermore, no matter what the intentions, drafts will always hit the poor and disadvantaged harder than those with greater means. For these reasons any effort to institute a draft should be vigorously opposed.

Ever since House Democrat Charles Rangel introduced his first proposal to bring back the military draft in 2003, it's been amazing to see how much amnesia there is on the subject, especially among some of those who consider themselves liberals or "progressives."

Rick Jahnkow, "Muddled Thinking About Conscription," *Draft Notices*, January–March 2007, published by the Committee Opposed to Militarism and the Draft. Reproduced by permission.

Shaky Premises

Supporters of Rangel's bill (which includes a mandatory civilian service option) make what seems on the surface to be a compelling case. They say one reason our government is so willing to launch aggressive military action is that the children of political leaders and the wealthy elite do not face much risk from combat. They point out that this is because the armed forces are maintained by a system of recruitment that unfairly targets working-class and middle-income people. They also argue that a stronger service ethic is needed, along with more civilian options for performing tasks that would benefit society. The points are valid, and so it seems reasonable when some people conclude that a system of conscription is needed to address such issues.

But the problem with this thinking is that it is far too simplistic and only focuses on limited parts of the picture. It ignores important historical facts and fails to consider an entirely different set of social and political consequences that are inherent in any system of involuntary service.

Whenever we go to war, whether our military is drafted or recruited, socio-economic status is always a factor in determining who is at greatest risk.

One of the forgotten historical facts is that whenever a draft has been employed in the U.S. (which has been infrequently), it has been used to make waging war possible, not as a device to keep our government from entering a conflict. A good example is our most recent experience with conscription during the Vietnam War. The draft that was already in place as the war developed made it easier for presidents Johnson and Nixon to merely open the tap and pour out more bodies to fuel the conflict. As a result, it lasted almost 10 years, took the lives of millions of people and caused massive destruction in Southeast Asia. All of this happened despite the strong anti-war and draft resistance movements that spread across the country.

No Draft Can Be Made Fair

Draft supporters say that in the past, the rules of the Selective Service System favored privileged youths and therefore didn't trigger the kind of opposition from the elite that would have stopped the Vietnam War sooner. But there is no evidence that drafting a few more affluent kids would have made a difference, since initial support for the war was high and was driven by a general Cold War fever that affected almost the entire population.

[A] system that would further militarize the U.S. is the last thing anyone should support.

The claim that a draft could be made fairer today isn't realistic anyway. There will always have to be medical deferments, which are easier to get when you have the money to pay for braces or private medical exams and documentation that are the key to getting disqualified at an Army induction physical. And those with a better education—which is linked to one's socio-economic status—will have a distinct advantage when it comes to successfully wading through the process to secure conscientious objector status. I know how these factors work because as a community college draft counselor during the Vietnam War, I struggled to help low-income students whose limited resources made it harder to gain recognition of legitimate claims for medical deferments and conscientious objector status. It won't be any different under Rangel's proposed draft. Furthermore, affluent individuals who do wind up in the military would still have the advantages of their education and political connections to help avoid combat.

Whenever we go to war, whether our military is drafted or recruited, socio-economic status is always a factor in determining who is at greatest risk. And in a system with a civilian service component like Rangel is proposing, advantages in education, personal wealth and political influence will still be a factor in avoiding the battlefield.

Drafts Militarize Society

Another part of the picture ignored by supporters of Rangel's legislation—one that is especially ironic for those draft advocates who say they are "peace activists"—is the increased militarization that comes with conscription. Because draftees are in the military for only two-year terms instead of four or six, there is a much higher turnover of personnel, and this means that a much larger portion of society is required to go through military training. One of the main functions of this training, especially at boot camp, is to strip the civilian identity from every trainee, instill in him or her the values of military culture, and perform the conditioning needed to produce an obedient soldier who is acclimated to the use of violence.

What many people ignore is that there is no comparable effort made to reverse this process when draftees leave the military. So even though the conditioning doesn't stick in everyone, the net effect over time is to further militarize civilian society, not civilianize the military (which some people have argued). Indeed, this militarization function is one reason why conscription has been so favored by authoritarian states. Examples include Nazi Germany, Imperial Japan, Prussia, and dictators like Napoleon, Stalin and Franco, just to name a few. In today's context of a U.S. government that wages preemptive war, threatens countries that have done nothing to harm us, and assumes police powers that the Constitution disallows, a system that would further militarize the U.S. is the last thing that anyone should support.

Imagine, for a moment, what would have happened if conscription had been in place at the time of 9/11. In that period of emotional nationalism, Bush could have easily gotten away with boosting draft calls and deploying a much larger force to the Middle East. Following the neocon agenda for the region, then, we could have already extended the fighting to Syria and Iran by now, and then moved on to a confrontation with North Korea.

Those Opposed to War Should Oppose A Draft

This leads me to point out a major contradiction in Rangel's rationale for a draft. He and others are arguing that it would help slow down the rush to war (a claim unsupported by any historical facts), while at the same time arguing that we need a draft because our military is exhausted and more troops are required for the mission they've been given. So which is it? Is a draft going to help prevent or end a war, or help wage it? And if it's the latter, then isn't opening up the tap for more troops the last thing that war opponents should want to do? If we really are against military aggression, isn't it better that we stick to demanding that the current mission be cancelled and, simultaneously, do everything we can to cut off the flow of personnel for war?

People who are now advocating a draft need to be challenged to look more closely at the facts and consider the full, global implications of what they are proposing.

If you believe the other part of Rangel's argument, he essentially wants to force a change in foreign policy by holding people's children hostage—which includes the children of people who have been struggling and sacrificing to end the Iraq war. Isn't hostage-taking something we generally condemn in our society, and shouldn't we have serious reservations about supporting such a tactic?

The reality is that popular opposition to bringing back the draft is still overwhelming, and legislators know that it would be political suicide to attempt such a thing at the moment. So why go to the trouble of rebutting pro-draft arguments from liberals or anyone else? The answer is that such efforts to promote conscription can, over time, accustom enough people to the idea of a draft that at a point in the future, in the context of some national emergency pretext, the politicians may then attempt what they now are afraid to do.

People who are now advocating a draft need to be challenged to look more carefully at the facts and consider the full, global implications of what they are proposing. Otherwise, they may eventually get what they are asking for, which would come back to haunt us all.

Organizations to Contact

The editors have compiled the following list of organizations concerned with the issues debated in this book. The descriptions are derived from materials provided by the organizations. All have publications or information available for interested readers. The list was compiled on the date of publication of the present volume; the information provided here may change. Be aware that many organizations take several weeks or longer to respond to inquiries, so allow as much time as possible.

American Civil Liberties Union
125 Broad Street, 18th Floor, New York, NY   10004
(212) 549-2585
Web site: www.aclu.org

The American Civil Liberties Union (ACLU) is a public advocacy organization that works with courts, legislatures, and communities to promote and protect personal liberties and related constitutional rights. Among its many interests is the equal treatment of gays and lesbians under the law. The ACLU opposes the military's policies on homosexuality as unfair and discriminatory. The organization provides press releases, policy and position statements, and/or legal *amicus* briefs (arguments submitted for a court's consideration by persons or entities who are not parties to the litigation, but who have a strong interest or concern in the subject matter at issue) for use in motions and appellate briefs in federal and state courts.

American Friends Service Committee
1501 Cherry Street, Philadelphia, PA   19102
(215) 241-7000 • fax: (215) 241-7275
Web site: www.afsc.org

The American Friends Service Committee (AFSC) is a non-profit organization originally founded by Quakers in 1917 to provide conscientious objectors with an alternative opportunity to aid civilian war victims. It continues its work to promote service to others, social justice, and peace programs around the world. The "Youth and Militarism" link found at its main Web site features several of its publications, including *Do You Know Enough to Enlist?* and *Questions for Military Recruiters.*

America Supports You
Web site: www.americasupportsyou.mil

American Supports You (ASY) is an organization sponsored by the U.S. Department of Defense that recognizes the support Americans feel for the men and women in the armed forces, and communicates that support to service members serving at home and abroad. Through its Web site, individuals can send messages of support to U.S. servicemen and women. The organization also serves as a resource to service members in need of assistance, directing them to various programs and organizations around the country that can provide them and their family members with resources and advice.

Coalition Against Militarism In Our Schools
P.O. Box 3012, South Pasadena, CA   91031
(626) 799-9118
e-mail: info@militaryfreeschools.org
Web site: www.militaryfreeschools.org

The Coalition Against Militarism In Our Schools (CAMS) is a non-profit program operating under the International Humanities Center, with a stated mission to demilitarize schools by presenting alternatives. CAMS has written a resolution approved by the California Federation of Teachers seeking to eliminate Section 9528 from any reauthorization of No Child Left Behind Act (which provides military access to all schools that accept federal funds) as applicable to California.

Committee Opposed to Militarism and the Draft
P.O. Box 15195, San Diego, CA   92175
(760) 753-7518

e-mail: COMD@comdsd.org
Web site: www.comdsd.org

The Committee Opposed to Militarism and the Draft (COMD) defines itself as an anti-militarism organization "that also challenges the institution of the military, its effect on society, its budget, its role abroad and at home, and the racism, sexism and homophobia that are inherent in the armed forces and Selective Service System." It directs its focus on community education, youth outreach, and direct action. Two of its related publications are *Teach Peace* and *High School Rights*.

National Association for Uniformed Services
5535 Hempstead Way, Springfield, VA   22151
(703) 750-1342 • fax: (703) 354-4380
e-mail: info@naus.org
Web site: www.naus.org

The National Association for Uniformed Services (NAUS) is the only military-affiliated association whose membership is open to all military branches and ranks, active and retired. It provides its members with assistance in all areas of military service, including recruitment, retention, spousal support, and survivorship. It also lobbies and promotes members' interests in Washington. NAUS publishes the *Uniformed Services Journal*.

National Priorities Project
17 New South Street, Northampton, MA   01060
(413) 584-9556 • fax: (413) 586-9647
e-mail: info@nationalpriorities.org
Web site: www.nationalpriorities.org

The National Priorities Project (NPP) is a non-profit research organization that analyzes and clarifies federal data for the general reading public. The organization focuses on issues involving federal budgets and spending, as well as other key policies affecting government at all levels. Military recruiting is one of the topics the group studies. Its publication *Military Recruiting—2006* examines trends in recruiting quantity, quality, and spending.

Project on Youth and Non-Military Opportunities
P.O. Box 230157, Encinitas, CA   92023
(760) 634-3604
e-mail: projyano@aol.com
Web site: www.projectyano.org

Project on Youth and Non-Military Opportunities (Project YANO) works in conjunction with the Committee Opposed to Militarism and the Draft (COMD), both of which are antimilitarist organizations working with schools to provide alternatives to the military for students and other youths. It produces numerous pamphlets on topics related to recruiting, such as "Military Enlistment," "Non-Military Alternatives," and "JROTC."

U.S. Armed Forces
(866) VIEW-NOW
Web site: www.todaysmilitary.com

The U.S. Armed Forces include the four active duty military services—the Army, Marines, Navy, and Air Force—their Reserves, the National Guard, and the Coast Guard. Together they are charged with defending the United States' vital interests at home and abroad. Every branch of the armed forces engages in its own publicity and recruiting activities, including Web sites, phone numbers, and publications. The U.S. Department of Defense maintains the "Today's Military" Web site as a clearinghouse of information on all branches of the armed forces, with the goal of educating "parents, teachers, and others about the opportunities and benefits available to young people in the Military today."

War Resisters League
339 Lafayette St., New York, NY   10012
(212) 228-0450 • fax: (212) 228-6193

e-mail: wrl@warresisters.org
Web site: www.warresisters.org

The War Resisters League (WRL) is a private organization committed to a philosophy of non-violence, democracy, and equality. It maintains a number of programs aimed at reducing or eliminating war and violence. This includes a Youth and Countermilitarism Program, which publishes the *DMZ: A Guide to Taking Your School Back From the Military* booklet.

Bibliography

Books

Beth Asch, Can Du, and Matthias Schonlau	*Policy Options for Military Recruiting in the College Market: Results from a National Survey.* Santa Monica, CA: RAND, 2004.
Ronald D. Fricker Jr. and C. Christine Fair	*Going to the Mines to Look for Diamonds: Experimenting with Recruiting Stations in Malls.* Santa Monica, CA: RAND, 2003.
Curtis L. Gilroy, Barbara A. Bicksler, and John T. Warner	*The All-Volunteer Force: Thirty Years of Service.* College Park, MD: Potomac Books, 2004.
Philip Gold	*The Coming Draft: The Crisis in Our Military and Why Selective Service Is Wrong for America.* New York: Presidio Press, 2006.
Bill Harris	*The Complete Idiot's Guide to Careers in the U.S. Military.* Indianapolis, IN: Alpha Publishers, 2002.
Max Hastings	*Warriors: Portraits from the Battlefield.* New York: Knopf, 2006.
James R. Hosek, et al.	*Attracting the Best: How the Military Competes for Information Technology Personnel.* Santa Monica, CA: RAND, 2004.

Kaplan	*Kaplan ASVAB, 2007 Ed.: The Armed Services Vocational Aptitude Battery,* rev. ed. New York: Kaplan Education, 2006.
J.F. Leahy	*Honor, Courage, Commitment: Navy Boot Camp.* Annapolis, MD: U.S. Naval Institute Press, 2002.
August T. Murray	*Military Recruiting: How to Build Recruiting Skills, Get Results, Adapt to the Mission, and Sustain Success.* Bloomington, IN: AuthorHouse, 2005.
Scott A. Ostrow	*Guide to Joining the Military.* Lawrenceville, NJ: Thomson/ARCO, 2004.
Kelly Perdew	*Take Command: 10 Leadership Principles I Learned in the Military and Put to Work for Donald Trump.* Washington, DC: Regnery Publishing, 2006.
Rod Powers and Jennifer Lawler	*ASVAB For Dummies,* 2nd ed. Indianapolis, IN: Wiley Publishing, 2007.
U.S. Department of Defense	*Americas Top Military Careers: Official Guide to Occupations in the Armed Forces,* 4th ed. Indianapolis, IN: Jist Publishing, 2003.

U.S. National Research Council, Committee on the Youth Population and Military Recruitment — *Attitudes, Aptitudes, and Aspirations of American Youth: Implications for Military Recruiting*, Eds. Paul Sacket and Anne Mavor. Washington, DC: National Academy Press, 2003.

Michael C. Volkin — *The Ultimate Basic Training Guidebook: Tips, Tricks, and Tactics for Surviving Boot Camp*, 2nd ed. New York: Savas Beatie, 2005.

Periodicals

Drake Bennet — "Doing Disservice," *American Prospect*, October 2003.

Michael Bronner — "Abuse by Military Recruiters," *Blade* (Toledo, OH), September 26, 2006.

"The Recruiters' War," *Vanity Fair*, September 2005.

Bruce Chapman — "A Bad Idea Whose Time is Past: The Case Against Universal Service," *Brookings Review*, Fall 2002.

Congressional Daily — "Dems Want Hearing on Mounting Recruiting Violations," September 12, 2006.

Brendan Conway — "Elites and the Military," *Washington Times*, September 5, 2006.

Diego Cupolo — "Military Recruiters in High Schools," *Gotham Gazette* (New York, NY), January 2007.

Thomas J. Cutler   "Someone Else's Turn," *U.S. Naval Institute Proceedings*, December 2006.

David Goodman   "NCLB Accesses High-Schoolers for the Military in War Time," *Education Digest*, May 2004.

Ken Harbaugh   "Commentary: Military Recruiters on Campus," *National Public Radio: All Things Considered*, November 25, 2005.

Lawrence Hardy   "Recruiters at School," *American School Board Journal*, October 2005.

Hartford Courant (CT)   "Don't Strong-Arm Recruits," August 28, 2006.

Bob Herbert   "Op-Ed: The Army's Hard Sell," *New York Times*, June 27, 2005.

Karen Houppert   "Who's Next?" *Nation*, September 12, 2005.

Tim Kane   "Who Are the Recruits?: The Demographic Characteristics of U.S. Military Enlistment, 2003–2005," Center for Data Analysis Report no. 06–09, *Heritage Foundation*, October 27, 2006.

Stanley Kurtz   "San Francisco to Army: Drop Dead," *Weekly Standard*, November 28, 2005.

Jorge Mariscal   "The Poverty Draft: Do Military Recruiters Disproportionately Target Communities of Color and the Poor?" *Sojourners*, June 2007.

Meredith May   "De-Recruiter Wins Long Haul Prize," *San Francisco Chronicle*, September 16, 2006.

Renae Merle   "Army Tries Private Pitch for Recruits," *Washington Post*, September 6, 2006.

Jack Minch   "Five Years After 9/11, Military Recruiters Busy," *The Sun* (Lowell, MA), September 15, 2006.

Brian Mockenhaupt   "The Army We Have," *Atlantic Monthly*, June 2007.

Officer   "Military Recruiters Still Face Barriers on Campus," May 2006.

Judy O'Rourke   "Military Recruiters Compete to Lure People," *Daily News* (Los Angeles), October 17, 2006.

Philadelphia Inquirer   "Military Recruiters on Campus: High Court Ruling Is On the Mark," March 8, 2006.

Stephen Phillips   "Let in the Army or Risk Your Funding," *Times Educational Supplement*, July 11, 2003.

James Pinkerton   "Immigrants Find Military a Faster Path to Citizenship," *Houston Chronicle*, September 14, 2006.

Reading Eagle (PA)   "Many Aren't Willing to Even Debate Draft," November 28, 2006.

Thom Shanker

"Army and Other Ground Forces Meet '06 Recruiting Goals," *New York Times*, October 10, 2006.

Barry Strauss

"Reflections on the Citizen-Soldier," *Parameters*, Summer 2003.

Stuart Tannock

"Is 'Opting Out' Really an Answer? Schools, Militarism, and the Counter-Recruitment Movement in Post-September 11 United States at War," *Social Justice*, vol. 32, no. 3, 2005.

Index